God and His Final Messenger

Medinan Period

Introduces the life of the Final Prophet and the main events that depict his role as the last Messenger of God on Earth. The attributes and sunnah of God (how He deals with human beings) will be introduced at appropriate places to illustrate how God intervenes in our lives, as He did in the Prophet's life. This level will cover the Medinan period.

Publisher © 2026 Ghamidi Center of Islamic Learning - Al-Mawrid US

Ghamidi Center of Islamic Learning

www.ghamidi.org   AN INITIATIVE OF AL-MAWRID US.

Publisher: Ghamidi Center of Islamic Learning - Al-Mawrid US
ISBN: 978-1-966600-27-5

Address: 3620 N Josey Ln, Suite 230 Carrollton, TX 75007
Website: www.ghamidicenter.com
Email: info@ghamidi.org

Chapter 1

Introduction to the Course

This chapter introduces the course and its objectives.

Introduction

- The Quran has made the obedience of Prophet Muhammad a condition for loving God and receiving His love and forgiveness (Surah 3, Verse 31).
- A hadith narrated by Anas ibn Malik implies that loving Prophet Muhammad reflects one's perfection of faith (Sahih Al-Bukhari 15, Muslim 44).
- Loving God and His messenger, and obeying them, are part of our religion. However, can we claim to have a deep, sincere love for someone without knowing them?
- This two-part course is unique in that it seeks to introduce God and His final messenger by studying the messenger's life on earth, known as Seerah. Through this course, we will learn how his life accurately depicted the Quranic teachings, how he lived, and how God manifested His being, commands, and practices through His final messenger. This way, we will learn relevant attributes of God as we study Seerah.
- Studying the Seerah of Prophet Muhammad and how God accompanied him throughout his life will help us build true love for him and his Lord, who is our Lord.
- The content of this course is drawn from the Quran and other authentic sources.
- The course is divided into two parts: the first will focus on the life of the Prophet Muhammad in Makkah until his migration to Medina, also known as the Makkan period.
- The second part of this course will focus on the life of Prophet Muhammad in Medina till his departure from this earth, also known as the Medinan period.

Course Objectives

- To get to know our God, Allah (the Most High), and His Final Messenger, Prophet Muhammad (Peace be upon him), through studying the life of the Messenger and how Allah helped him throughout the mission given to him as a Messenger.

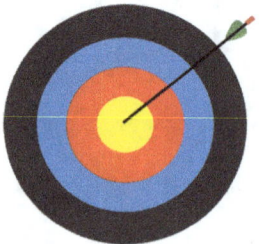

- Describe the key events in the life of Prophet Muhammad after he was made a messenger while he lived in Makkah.
- Understand how a messenger and his companions go through different stages and the challenges of the mission until they complete it.

What is Seerah?

In the Arabic language, it comes from the word "Sara," which means to be on a journey

- Seerah is an area of Islamic knowledge where we study the life of Prophet Muhammad:
    - His biography.
    - Events related to his life.
    - Events related to his mission.
    - His relationships as a human being.
    - His habits, preferences, likes, dislikes.
    - And many other aspects of his life.
- His companions tried to preserve his life history, which reached us through narrations called Hadith.
- The Quran also tells us some parts of the life of Prophet Muhammad, but not the complete life.

Important

The primary source of Seerah is Ahadith.

Hadith: A collection of the sayings, actions, and approvals of the Prophet and any matter related to his life reported by the people around him. Ahadith is the plural of Hadith.

What is Hadith?

- Prophet Muhammad's companions lived with him, talked to him, saw him, observed him, asked him questions, spent day and night with him, and then some of them recorded them so they could benefit from them later.

- Some of these people (red and orange in color in the picture below) will go out and recount all this to others who were not present.

- These people narrate their stories to others, and this continues. This knowledge base is Hadith.

- Historians took these narrations from different times, compiled them, and verified them to some extent

- Later historians also benefit from the work of individual narrators and previous historians.

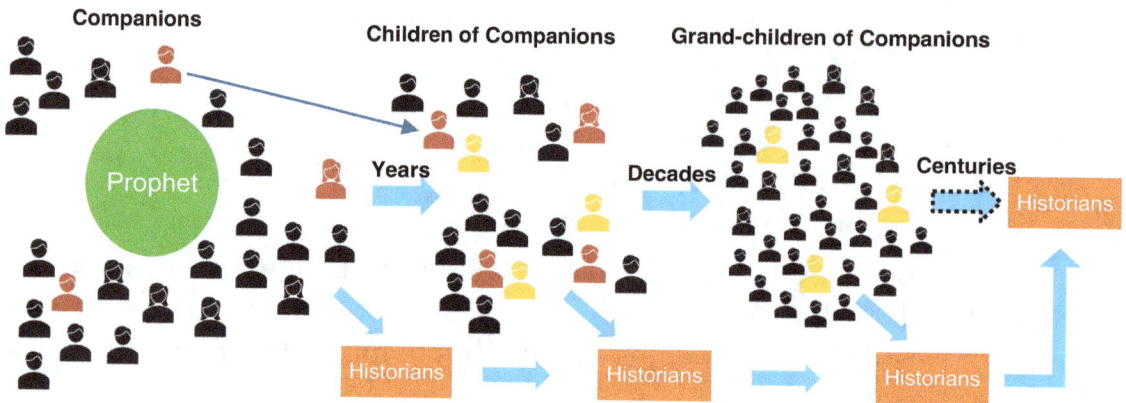

Knowing how narrations were transmitted, it is possible that something was not transmitted correctly or that someone fabricated something about the Prophet. Do you know what the early scholars of Islam did to handle this problem?

Importance of studying the Seerah

The importance

- It is natural to want to know more about the person whom we claim to love.
- It increases our love for him, which is required for our faith.
- In the Quran, events are briefly mentioned, but the Seerah provides more detail.
- We learn from his life and moral behavior and try our best to emulate them.
- The more we know about him, the more we can educate people around us about his character.

Aisha reported: "Verily, the character of the Prophet of Allah was the Quran."
(Sahih Muslim 746)

Our relationship with the Prophet

- Our relationship with the Prophet is: Believe, love, and obey. The Quran described this relationship in this beautiful verse:

قُلْ إِنْ كُنْتُمْ تُحِبُّونَ اللّٰهَ فَاتَّبِعُونِي يُحْبِبْكُمُ اللّٰهُ وَ يَغْفِرْ لَكُمْ ذُنُوْبَكُمْ

Say, (O Muhammad to Muslims), if you really love Allah, then follow me; Allah will love you and will forgive your sins (3:31)

- Prophet Muhammad is now the only source of guidance from Allah.
- It is our duty and part of our faith to learn and understand how Allah and His final messenger want us to live our daily lives.
- This life is a test of our moral character, and Prophet Muhammad's character is the best example for us.
- The best way to earn the pleasure of Allah and become closer to Him is through following the Prophet.

The phases of Prophet's Life

- The life of Prophet Muhammad can be divided into three distinct phases:
  - Before prophethood
  - Makkan period
  - Medinan period
- Although as Muslims we look at his life after he was made a Prophet of God, his life before Prophethood is equally important to study.
- When reading the Quran, we can easily notice that the message and themes of the Quranic Surahs differ between the Makkan and Medinan periods.
- His challenges and enemies in Makkah and Medina were also very different.

Prophet Muhammad's Age = 63 Years

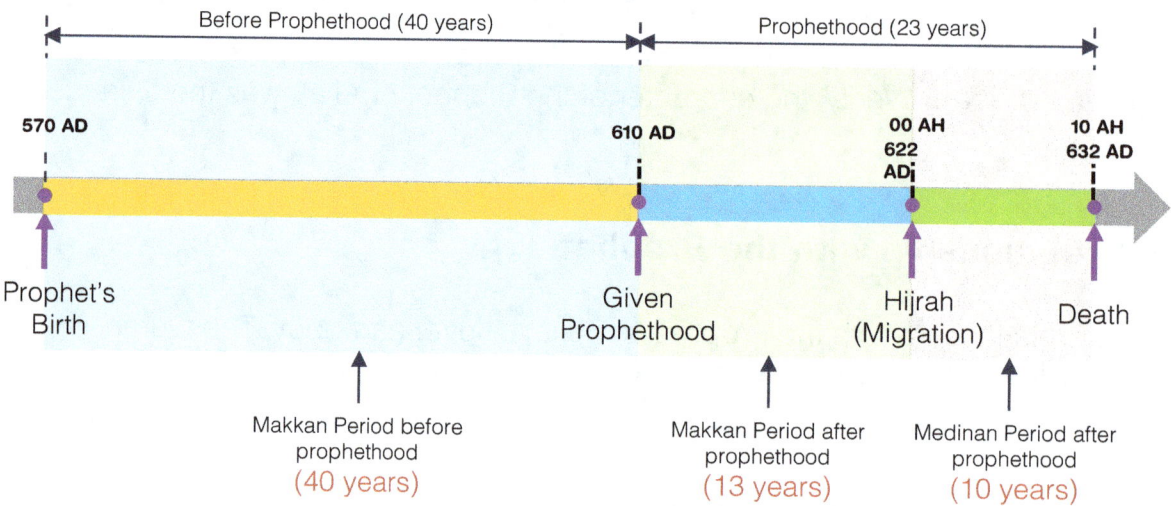

In Level 3, we will study the Medinan period of the Prophet's life. This includes around 10 years after Prophethood until he passes from this world.

God: His attributes and practices

The Compassionate	**The Most Merciful**	**The Just**
The Wise	**The Grateful**	**The Reckoner**
The Responder	**The Protector**	**The Great**

The Quran clearly states about God:

There is nothing that resembles Him (in this world) (42:11)

- As mentioned in the introduction, in this course, we will learn about our God, Allah, and His attributes.
- We do not know Allah's physical person (his being); we can only know Him through His attributes.
- The best way to know God is to see how He deals with us and this world. This is visible through His attributes.
- The Prophet went through many phases and faced many hardships throughout his life, but God always remained with him in every difficult time.
- God showed His attributes and practices throughout the life of Prophet Muhammad.
- We face many difficulties and challenges in our modern lives. By learning about what the Prophet Muhammad did in the face of adversity, challenges, rejection, grief, and loss, we can find answers and strategies to cope. Our circumstances may be very different from those of that time, but we can still find many inspirations for modern life in the Prophet's example and take practical lessons from it.
- Similarly, Prophet's life is the best way to gain a clear understanding of God's attributes and to build a strong relationship with Him.

Activities

Throughout this course, you will complete various activities called the **Seerah Activity**. These activities must be completed and submitted to the teacher in class on the due date.

Important notes

- Throughout the course, the words God and Allah are used interchangeably.
- For brevity and editing, the salutations for the Prophet Muhammad, PEACE BE UPON HIM, are not repeated. But it is highly encouraged that whenever we say or read his name, we send him salutations.

Class instructions

- You are required to attend all classes unless you have a valid reason to skip.
- Please send a note (or ask your parents) to your teacher on Google Classroom if you will skip a session.
- Attendance will be taken at the beginning of every class. Arriving in class 5 minutes after the start will be counted as tardy.
- Three (3) tardies will be counted as one absence.
- Attendance will be counted toward your final assessment.
- Every student will be assessed via:
    - Participation in the class
    - Multiple Quizzes
    - Assignments
    - Semester Exam
    - End-of-Year Exam

We all love Prophet Muhammad, but we also idealize other people (alive or historical) in our lives. Share a short paragraph with the class about the person you look up to, other than Prophet Muhammad.

Chapter 2

Arrival in Medina

In this chapter, we will review the arrival of Muslims in Medina and the factors that led to it before we begin the study of the Medinan period of Prophethood.

Medinan Phase of Prophethood
(10 years)

Quiz

Do you remember why Prophet Muhammad and Muslims left Makkah?

A New Home in Yathrib (Medina)

Why did Prophet Muhammad leave Makkah?

Makkah   **Medina**

1. Prophet Muhammad claimed Prophethood at the age of 40 to revive the message of Prophet Ibrahim, i.e., ISLAM.
2. The Quraysh considered Islam a direct threat to their religious leadership, which was also the source of their economic activities.
3. The Prophet was accused of being a poet, magician, sorcerer, and a mad person.
4. Muslims in Makkah were going through the worst period of religious oppression at the hands of tribal leaders.
5. Many early Muslims, especially those who were financially and socially weak, were tortured and killed at the hands of tribal leaders.
6. The tribe and the larger family of Prophet Muhammad were socially and economically boycotted.
7. The leaders were making it difficult for the Prophet to give out the message of Islam to anyone visiting Makkah for Hajj and other reasons.
8. The leaders of the Quraysh became harsher on Muslims day by day, and the Prophet had the responsibility to save his fellow Muslims from the most brutal of punishments just because of their religion.
9. The Quraysh had surrounded his house and were ready to kill him – God saved him miraculously.
10. The Prophet did not migrate to Medina of his own free will.
11. God asked him to move to a new place as part of his mission as a messenger.

Yathrib – the old Medinah

- Yathrib was about as far as a ten-day journey north of Makkah.
- It was more multi-ethnic and multi-cultural than Makkah.
- Idol worship was not as extreme here.
- Yathrib was renamed Medinah after Prophet Muhammad migrated there.
- It was named "Medina tun Nabi" (The city of the Prophet). Later, it is reduced to Medina.

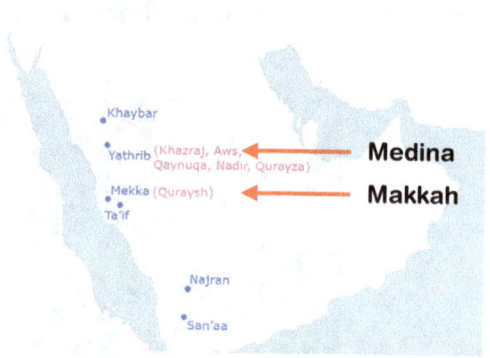

Pagan Tribes

- Two pagan Arab tribes, the Aws and the Khazraj, had lived there for a long time. They were idolaters with the same roots as Quraysh.

Jewish Tribes

- Three main tribes: Banu Nadir, Banu Qurayzah, Banu Qaynuqah.
- Migrated from Palestine in search of the last prophet, which they thought would come in their generation.
- Banu Nadir and Qurayzah were scholars of the Torah.

Relationship between Jews and Idolators

- Aws and Khazraj were idolaters but knew Tawheed and the Day of Judgment. Some of them even accepted Judaism.
- People of the Book (especially Jews) who were aware of the revelation and considered more knowledgeable had great influence in this area because of their superiority.
- Jews were politically very active there, in a negative way, and plotted to damage Aws and Khazraj from the inside to keep hold of the area.
- When some leaders of Aws and Khazraj tried to resist this influence, it led to many battles between the two, resulting in human and financial losses.
- This resulted in the loss of key leadership on both sides, and there was no one to stand up against the Jews; both tribes realized this later and looked for new leadership.

Awa and Khazraj wanted to break away from Jewish influence.

Reaction of the People of Yathrib

- The Prophet and his companion, Abu Bakr, reached Quba/Qiba, situated outside of Medina.
- It was a festive occasion in Quba, and the people opened their hearts to the Prophet.
- A man saw from a hill that some travelers were on their way. He said aloud, "O' People, he for whom you were waiting has arrived."
- Many people mistook Abu Bakr for the Prophet. Later, when Abu Bakr used his cloth sheet to cover the Prophet from the sun, they realized their mistake.
- The Jews in this area also came to meet the Prophet, and after meeting him, they went back and confirmed that this was the same Prophet who was foretold in their books, but they could not accept him and would oppose him.
- The people of Yathrib were hopeful that by accepting Islam and Prophet Muhammad as their prophet, they would gain the upper hand over the Jews and get rid of their submissive situation.
- He laid the foundation of the first mosque after the revival of Islam, Masjid-e-Quba.

Masjid Al-Quba
(the first mosque of Islam after Prophet Muhammad)

- It is regarded as the **first mosque in Islamic history** that was established by Prophet Muhammad.
- Its first stone is said to have been laid by the Prophet himself, and the structure completed by his companions. He participated in building it.
- The mosque was repeatedly modified and expanded over time. It was expanded under Caliph Usman. Another expansion occurred in 684 CE, during the reign of the Umayyad caliph Abdul Malik Al-Marwan. Under his successor, Al-Walid, the mosque was rebuilt. Its first minaret was added during the reign of Umar bin Abdul Aziz (Wikipedia)

Yathrib became Al-Medinah

Yathrib ➡ Medina

- The camel of the Prophet finally stopped at a place that belonged to Banu Malik Al-Najjar. The Prophet stayed at an adjacent house that belonged to Abu Ayyub Ansari for the next seven months.
- The Prophet did not like bad names. He changed the names of many companions because their names were somehow associated with polytheistic beliefs.
- The same thing happened with Yathrib. When he arrived here, he changed the city's name because the word Yathrib carries a negative connotation of blame.
- He changed the name to "Al-Medinat un Nabi," "the City of the Prophet," which became Medinah in short.
- In many narrations attributed to the Prophet, the virtues of Medinah are described, indicating that God chose this city for the Prophet and Islam. According to one narration, he started seeing this city in his dreams one year before the migration.

Prophet's love for the city of Medinah

- In Sahih Bukhari, it's narrated that the Prophet made dua for Madinah: "O Allah, cause us to love Madinah as much as we love Makkah, or even more."
- The Prophet also made dua that Madinah be blessed — he said, "O Allah, give us barakah ... in this city of ours." And in Bukhari, he said, "O Allah, Your servant Ibrahim declared Makkah a Haram; and I too am Your servant, so I make dua that You make Madinah a Haram."
- And Ibn Abbas narrates that whenever the Prophet returned from an expedition and saw the line of Madinah in the distance, he would become excited and tell his camel or horse to go faster.

A new reality

- Prophet Muhammad and his companions were facing a new reality in Medina. Medinah was more multi-ethnic and multi-cultural.
- A new dimension of dealing with the People of the Book was added to the already complex situation in Medinah.
- The Prophet spent 13 years in Makkah, and he and his companions were about to start a new phase in the history of Islam. They were about to lay the foundation for the first Islamic state of Medina, which expanded across many continents in less than 20 years. Muslims and their civilization ruled the world for over 1200 years afterward.

What are the benefits and challenges of moving to a new place? If you have had one, share your experience.

The Protector (Friend)

- At its core, it means the true "Protective Friend," signifying that He manages all affairs, protects believers, and is intimately close to His creation, guiding them from darkness to light.
- That's how a true friend must be in this life.
- When Allah befriends someone and protects them, then He finds ways to help that we cannot even imagine.
- Getting an ally in Medina and protection through their residents is an excellent example of how Allah helped the Muslims

إِنَّ اللّٰهَ لَهٗ مُلْكُ السَّمٰوٰتِ وَ الْاَرْضِ ۚ يُحْىٖ وَ يُمِيْتُ ۚ وَ مَا لَكُمْ مِّنْ دُوْنِ اللّٰهِ مِنْ وَّلِيٍّ وَّ لَا نَصِيْرٍ

(O believers) Indeed, to Allah belongs the dominion of the heavens and the earth; He gives life and causes death. And you have no protector or helper besides Allah. (9:116)

Chapter 3

Building Al-Masjid An-Nabawi

In this chapter, we will talk about one of the defining moments in Muslims' lives, which is the building of the Al-Masjid An-Nabawi, which played a critical role in the mission of Prophet Muhammad.

Construction of the Mosque

First thing first

- Laying the foundation of a mosque was the first thing the Prophet did upon his arrival. The mosque played a critical role in his prophethood.

- As he settled into the new place, the Prophet laid the foundation of the mosque that we now know as Al-Masjid An-Nabawi.

- There was a spacious land with a few graves and date palms next to where the Prophet stayed. The Prophet bought it from the two orphans who owned it.

- Muslims participated in the construction with the Prophet while making this dua: "O God! There is no benefit other than the benefit of the Hereafter, so forgive the Muhajirun and the Ansar."

- The mosque was built with unbaked bricks; the pillars were made from the trunks of date palm trees, and the roof was made from their branches and leaves. Pebbles were laid out on the mosque's floor.

- The Prophet himself participated in the construction of the mosque.

- There was no pulpit at first, and the Prophet used to lean against the tree trunk. Later, a woman asked her slave to make a pulpit for the mosque.

- To the east were small rooms where the Prophet lived.

How did Adhan start?

The Muslims discussed several ways to invite people to attend daily prayers at the mosque. They thought of the practices of the Jews and Christians, such as sounding bells, but they did not feel satisfied. It is said that either Abdullah Bin Zayd or Umar (or both) heard the words of the Adhan in their dreams and told the Prophet. The Prophet said: "Insha'Allah, this is a true dream." Then he instructed Bilal to recite the Adhan loudly while standing on a high place so that it could be heard in distant areas.

The role of Al-Masjid An-Nabawi

The association of the people with the mosque was such that the city later grew into an almost ring-shaped form, centering on the mosque.

- It is important to note that as soon as he migrated from Makkah and reached new places like Quba and Yathrib, he first built mosques. This shows the importance of mosques in our lives. The mosques are called the Houses of Allah.

- At the time, the Prophet had 2 wives: Sawda and Aisha. Both of their houses were built next to the masjid.

- The mosque was the center of all religious and sometimes social and political activities:
  - Five daily prayers and Friday prayers.
  - Meeting the Prophet for consultation on different religious and family matters.
  - Learn about Islam and accept Islam.
  - Meeting various tribes and other foreign delegations who want to learn about Islam or negotiate a pact or other matters.
  - When something important or urgent needs to be shared with the community, Adhan will be called out to gather in the mosque, and the Prophet would then address them and discuss it.
  - Marriages (Nikah) were conducted. This became a Sunnah later, and Muslims now perform their Nikah in mosques.
  - Preparing and planning for the wars.
  - People who do not have a home or other places to stay will stay outside the mosque.

"Prayer in this mosque of mine is better than a thousand prayers in any other mosque, except the Sacred Mosque (Masjid Al-Haram in Makkah). Prayer in the Sacred Mosque is one hundred times better than prayer in this mosque of mine." (Musnad Ahmad 15685)

Al-Masjid An-Nabawi

Total area: **59 acres (1 acre = 43560 sq ft.)**
Number of minarets: **10**
Number of doors: **85**
Number of Domes: **167**
Number of sliding domes: **27**
Total number of pillars: **4600**
Number of lighting points: **21,520**
Number of Chandeliers: **305**
Number of retractable Umbrellas: **12**
Number of people it can serve: **1.8 million**

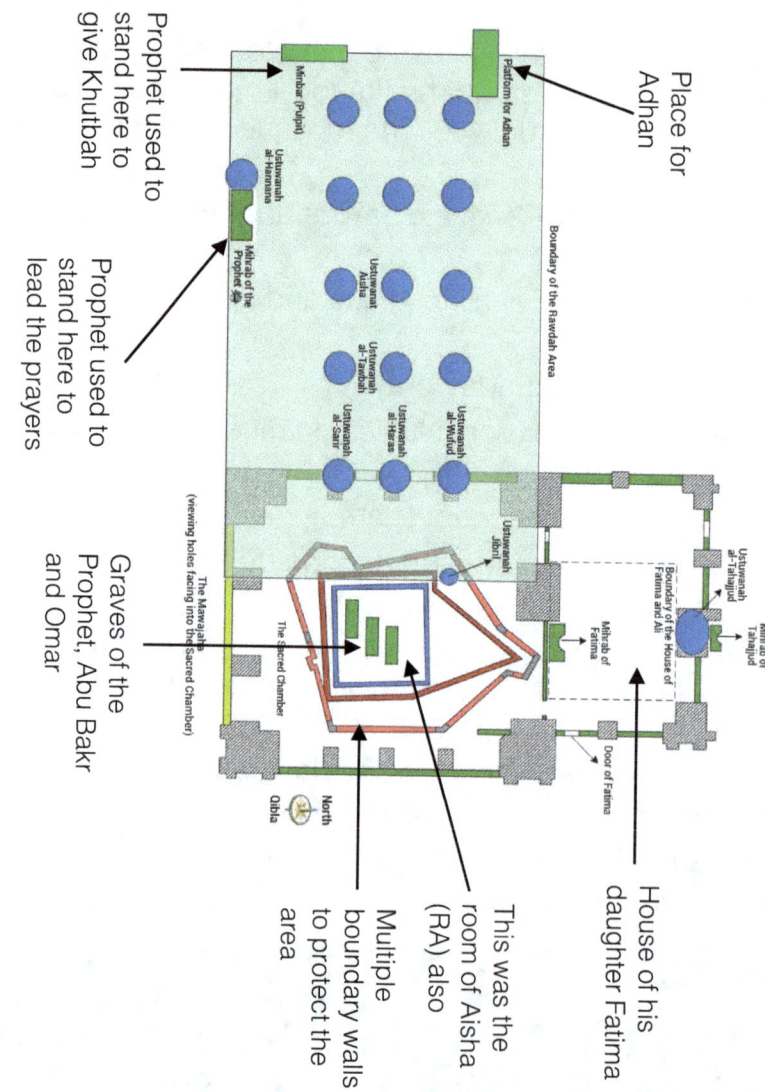

Prophet used to stand here to give Khutbah

Prophet used to stand here to lead the prayers

Graves of the Prophet, Abu Bakr and Omar

Multiple boundary walls to protect the area

This was the room of Aisha (RA) also

House of his daughter Fatima

Place for Adhan

The role of mosque in a Muslim Community

The mosque plays a very comprehensive role in the lives of Muslims.

Place of worship	Friday Prayers	Community Center
Political center	Islamic Education	Memorizing Quran
Reading Quran	Breaking Fast Together	Lectures/Talks
Brotherhood / Sisterhood	Social Activities	Taraweeh Prayer
New Muslims	Charity Programs	Eid Celebrations
Help each other		

The mosque brings the Muslim community together. To remain good Muslims, understand our religion well, and play a positive and healthy role in our community, we must stay connected to our local mosques.

What activities does your mosque have, and what role does it play in your life?

God is Greater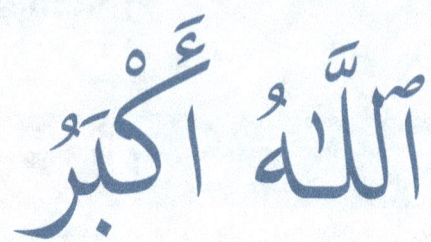

- It means "God is Greater than Everything". Meaning He is Exalted above everything.
- It is meant to celebrate life, happy occasions, achievements, and any good that happens to us in this life.
- It's a statement to admit that God in our lives is greater than every good that is given to us and every good that we achieve.
- We repeat this in our daily prayers many times because it's a constant reminder that God is greater than anything we are thinking about during the prayers.
- Muslims and non-Muslims alike have misused this beautiful statement, and we should be aware of that.

وَ قُلِ الْحَمْدُ لِلّٰهِ الَّذِىْ لَمْ يَتَّخِذْ وَلَدًا وَّ لَمْ يَكُنْ لَّهٗ شَرِيْكٌ فِى الْمُلْكِ وَ لَمْ يَكُنْ لَّهٗ وَلِىٌّ مِّنَ الذُّلِّ وَ كَبِّرْهُ تَكْبِيْرًا

[Continue to show discipline in this prayer] and proclaim: Gratitude is for God Who neither has children nor is anyone His partner in His kingdom, nor does He need any helper in times of helplessness, and declare His exaltedness the way it should be. (17:111)

MASJID-E-NABAWI ALBUM

Create a digital album documenting the history of the MASJID-E-NABAWI and its various phases of construction over time through pictures and a brief description.

Instructions

- Use any digital platform, such as Canva or Google Slides, to create the Album.

- Ensure that an acknowledgment or reference is included for copyrighted material.

- Add key information related to the picture, accompanied by a brief description.

- The number of photos in the album should be between 5 and 8.

Chapter 4

The System of Brotherhood

In this chapter, we will study the system of brotherhood that Prophet Muhammad created upon arrival in Medina to solve the issue of settling emigrants from Makkah in Medina.

The Prophet's Marriage to Aisha (RA)

It is reported in a narration that the Prophet saw a dream about Aisha in which he was told that Aisha is his wife in this world and the Hereafter. **(Sahih Bukhari #3606)**

- In those days, it was pretty common for men to marry more than one woman.
- After Khadijah's death, the Prophet married Saudah because he had young children in the house.
- The marriage between people from two different tribes was an effective way to forge bonds in a tribal society.
- The Nikah between the Prophet and Aisha (the daughter of Abu Bakr) was formalized while they were still in Makkah, after the death of Khadijah.
- Aisha did not move to the Prophet's house at that time due to the situation of migration.
- After the migration, the Prophet did not bring Aisha immediately due to financial difficulties.
- He took out a loan to fulfill this responsibility, and finally, Aisha moved into one of the quarters next to the mosque.

Aisha Bint Abi Bakr

- According to some historians, Aisha was 16 at the time of her marriage and 19 when she moved into the Prophet's house. Based on historical records, this seems to be the most authentic report.
- She was the daughter of Abu Bakr, the Prophet's closest companion and the first Caliph, and is one of the most influential figures in early Islamic history.
- Known as Umm al-Muminin ("Mother of the Believers"), she was a prolific scholar, political leader, and a primary source for understanding the Prophet's personal life and teachings.
- She narrated thousands of Ahadith from Prophet Muhammad.
- She is described in Islamic tradition as the Prophet's most beloved wife after Khadija. It is narrated that Muhammad died in her arms and was buried in her room.

Settling in the new community

The Community of Medinah

- After the Prophet moved to Medina, the following groups made up the community, and the Prophet needed to work at every level to familiarize himself with the situation and build strong working relationships with all of them.

The Immigrants

- People migrating from Makkah were called **Al-Muhajiroon**.
- Some brought their savings, others left everything.
- Some were in dire straits.
- They had no place to live or anything to eat.

Muslim Ansar

- People living in Medina from the tribes of Aws and Khazraj who accepted Islam.
- They were called **'Ansar,'** which means 'helpers.'
- They made efforts to bring the Prophet to Medina.
- Prime supporters of the Muslims in Medina.

Jews

- The three main Jewish tribes lived in the suburbs of Medina.
- They were the direct addressees of the Quran.
- They were considered religiously 'educated' and had a big influence in the area.
- There were some Jews among the tribes of Aws and Khazraj as well.
- Aws and Khazraj are now comprised of Muslims, Jews, and Idolaters.

Other Tribes

- Many small and large tribes around Medina had relations with the Aws and the Khazraj.
- They were political allies of Aws and Khazraj and always helped them against any attack from outside.
- The Quraysh were planning to reach out to them to create problems for the Prophet.

The Challenges of Migration

- Some migrants were able to bring their belongings and savings, while others could not.
- Some of them have close or extended families in Medina, but others have no one they know in the city.
- All needed time to familiarize themselves with the area's cultural, social, and economic activities before they could play an active role in society.
- All of them immediately needed a roof over their heads, with no concept of 'renting'.
- The number of migrants increased over time as more and more people joined the Prophet.
- The society was unaware of mutual support and help beyond familial and tribal connections.
- Migrants with business skills may not be able to immediately start their own businesses due to a lack of funding or familiarity with existing market conditions.
- Some people got separated from their families (the women and children were left behind) in the process, and were emotionally disturbed.
- For any society to survive, grow, and develop, there must be a strong bond among its people, and that was completely missing from this new community right after the migration.

If you were put in charge of a situation involving migrants in your neighborhood, coming from a different country, what solutions would you recommend to help them adjust to this new environment? Be creative but practical.

The system of brotherhood (*Mu'akha*)

The solution

- Prophet Muhammad took an unusual social and economic initiative that was critical to the survival and stability of the early Muslim community in Medina. This was never done before in any community.
- Prophet Muhammad established a one-to-one bond between a Muhajir and an Ansar – that is, one Ansar would take care of one Muhajir.
- This arrangement continued for new migrants arriving in Medina.
- As migrants settled, they began taking care of their brothers and sisters from Makkah.
- The process of migration stopped after the victory of Makkah.

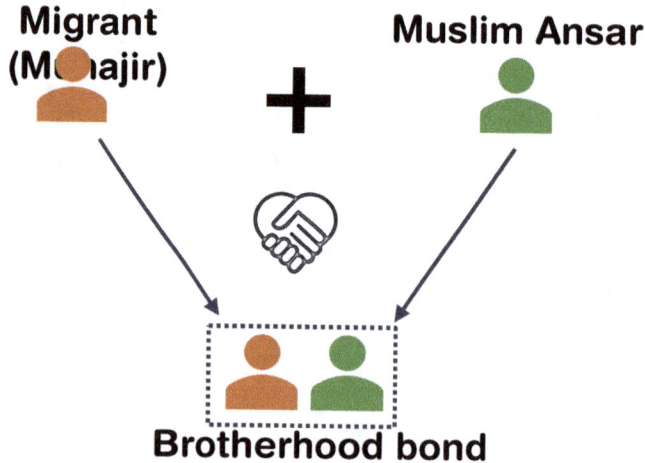

"Do not keep any grudge among yourselves; do not envy each other; do not turn away your face from each other; O servants of God! Be brothers to each other." (Hadith)

A community can overcome any challenge if everyone

The System

- The responsibility of the Ansar was:
  - Take the migrant brother under his protection as part of the tribal rule.
  - Accommodate his migrant brother, since it was not possible to build new settlements for the migrants.
  - Help and support him until he can start earning on his own.
- The migrants were also asked not to become an unnecessary burden on their Ansar brothers and to do their best to become independent as soon as practically possible.
- Ansar were so generous and loving towards the migrants that they sacrificed their own needs to meet their brothers' needs.
- The Quran praised the generosity of the Ansar and presented their character as a model to be emulated.

Example Brotherhoods

Migrant	Ansar	Ansar Tribe
Abu Bakr	Kharijah Bin Zuhayr	Khazraj
Umar Bin Al-Khattab	Utbah Bin Malik	Khazraj
Uthman Bin Affan	Aws Bin Thabit	Khazraj
Abu Ubaydah Bin Al Jarrah	Saad Bin Muad	Aws
Zubair Bin Al Awwam	Salmah Bin Salamah	Aws
Abul Rahman Bin Awf	Saad Bin Ar Rabee	Khazraj
Hamza Bin Abdul Muttalib	Zaid Bin Thabit	Khazraj
Abu Dharr Ghaffari	Mundhir Bin Amru	Khazraj
Musab Bin Umair	Abu Ayyub Ansari	Khazraj
Zaid Bin Haritha	Usaid Bin Hadheer	Aws
Muawiyyah Bin Abi Sufyan*	Hattat Bin Yazid	Aws

*Muawiyyah Bin Abi Sufyan reached Medinah many years after initial migration

Quran Praised the Ansar

- There are many verses of the Quran in which God praised the Ansar's generosity and their sacrifice for this great mission of Prophet Muhammad.

اِنَّ الَّذِيْنَ اٰمَنُوْا وَ هَاجَرُوْا وَ جَاهَدُوْا بِاَمْوَالِهِمْ وَ اَنْفُسِهِمْ فِيْ سَبِيْلِ اللّٰهِ وَ الَّذِيْنَ اٰوَوْا وَّ نَصَرُوْا اُولٰٓئِكَ بَعْضُهُمْ اَوْلِيَآءُ بَعْضٍ

"Indeed, those who have believed and emigrated and fought with their wealth and lives in the cause of God and those who gave shelter and aided them are protectors of each other." **(Anfal:72)**

وَ الَّذِيْنَ تَبَوَّؤُ الدَّارَ وَ الْاِيْمَانَ مِنْ قَبْلِهِمْ يُحِبُّوْنَ مَنْ هَاجَرَ اِلَيْهِمْ وَ لَا يَجِدُوْنَ فِيْ صُدُوْرِهِمْ حَاجَةً مِّمَّآ اُوْتُوْا وَ يُؤْثِرُوْنَ عَلٰٓى اَنْفُسِهِمْ وَ لَوْ كَانَ بِهِمْ خَصَاصَةٌ وَ مَنْ يُّوْقَ شُحَّ نَفْسِهٖ فَاُولٰٓئِكَ هُمُ الْمُفْلِحُوْنَ

"And those who, before them, had homes [in Medinah] and had adopted the Faith, love those who emigrate to them, and have no jealousy in their hearts for that which they have been given, and give them [emigrants] preference over themselves, even though they needed that. And whosoever is saved from his own greediness, such are they who will be successful." (Hashr:9)

Some Examples

- Abdul Rahman Bin Awf was made brother to Saad Bin Al Rabee. Saad offered to divide his property, land, and wealth into two portions.
- Abdul Rahman was a good businessman in Makkah. He thanked Saad and asked him to show him the market, and asked a few questions about the market situation and raw materials.
- Abdul Rahman established his business quickly and was able to stand on his own feet.
- Some Ansar tried to give a portion of their orchards to their migrant brothers. When the Prophet learned of it, he asked them not to do it.
- The migrants suggested that Ansar should remain the owner of the orchards and that migrants should work in them and earn a living.
- Some Ansar wanted to gift their houses and land to migrant brothers (as part of inheritance), but the Quran and the Prophet Muhammad stopped them.
- The Quran reminded them that only blood relations have the right of inheritance.

The Wisdom of Brotherhood

- In charity and good work, only a few people contribute – it is always challenging to convince everyone to participate and share the burden and reward.
- When a large number of people move to a place from another location, the original residents may feel pressure and develop a dislike towards the newcomers.
- It is easy for some people to incite such feelings and cause two groups to fight each other, leading to the creation of conspiracies.
- It was possible that when both migrants and Ansar compete for the opportunities available in society, the Ansar might start feeling hatred towards the migrants.
- It appears that the need for brotherhood arose more for social than economic reasons.

The Benefits of Brotherhood

- It distributed the burden on a larger number of people. Everyone felt they were working for the community's good.
- All the dangers associated with groupings were minimized. It created a special bond and trust among people rather than forming groups.
- Every Ansar had someone to teach them Islam and the Quran.
- The motivation for doing this was pure: to earn God's pleasure.
- The brotherhood began in the early Madani phase, but this relationship went a long way, even after the Conquest of Makkah and the Prophet's death.
- As we said, for any society to grow and develop, there must be a strong bond among its people. And the strongest of bonds is a bond of religion.
- This is a neglected sunnah of Prophet Muhammad because today, when we have new Muslims in the community, or when people migrate from other cities or countries to our community, they struggle in the new place. By reviving this sunnah, we can easily improve their situation.

The People of As-Suffah

- With so many migrants, it was not possible to immediately form a brotherhood for everyone for many reasons.
- A public shelter with the name "**As-Suffah**" was built outside the mosque.
- Some people even decided to stay in the shelter for extended periods – they were often called "the people of the shelter" (**Ashab us Suffah**).

SHELTER

- They were spending more time in the mosque with the Prophet, learning about Islam.
- Many narrations describe the difficulties these people faced as they chose to sacrifice the comfort of home for the opportunity to spend time with the Prophet.
- The famous narrator, Abu Huraira, was among those people.
- The Prophet took extra care of these people. Whenever he received food (such as fruit from an orchard), he would first share it with the people at the shelter.
- The number of people staying at the shelter ranged from 5 or 10 to up to 70.

Lessons Learned

We have many lessons to learn from Ansar's great acts of generosity and the migrants' response.

- ✓ The best way to deal with a crisis is to work toward the solution as a community.
- ✓ People who move from other places should be welcome, and we should make this migration as easy as possible for them.
- ✓ In exceptional circumstances like these, we should actively participate and help the community as much as possible.
- ✓ However, even in these special circumstances, when performing an act of charity, we should be aware of our blood relatives' rights to us.
- ✓ Our blood relatives have the most right to our inheritance and our wealth.
- ✓ People who are the beneficiaries of that charitable act should not become a burden on society and take undue advantage of it – they should benefit enough to become independent as quickly as possible.

Most Grateful

- When we do good, it's not just the people who appreciate it; Allah tells us that He appreciates it too.
- It is an honor for us that the King of the kings appreciates our good deeds and is grateful for them.
- That's why He chose one of the names for Himself, the Most Grateful.
- As a show of appreciation, Allah praised Muhajiroon and Ansar in the Quran and promised them the best reward in this life and in the Hereafter.
- We should also be grateful to God for His generosity and all the blessings He has given us.
- Prophet Muhammad said in a beautiful hadith:

"Whosoever relieves a believer of some grief related to this world, Allah will relieve him of some grief in the Hereafter. Whosoever removes the difficulties of a needy person who cannot pay his debt, Allah will remove his difficulties in this world and the Hereafter. Whosoever conceals the faults of a Muslim, Allah will conceal his faults in this world and the Hereafter. Allah will aid a servant (of His) so long as the servant aids his brother." **[Muslim]**

وَ مَنْ يَقْتَرِفْ حَسَنَةً نَّزِدْ لَهُ فِيهَا حُسْنًا إِنَّ اللّٰهَ غَفُورٌ شَكُورٌ

And say: A person who does a virtue, We shall increase His goodness for him in his virtue. There is no doubt that God is very Forgiving and Grateful (through acceptance and reward). (42:23)

BROTHERHOOD CARDS

Create "Brotherhood Cards" that highlight two to three key attributes or qualities of the two Sahabis between whom the Prophet formed the brotherhood.

Example Pair

Abu Bakr (RA)

1) Quality #1
2) Quality #2
3) Attribute or something important about him.

Kharijah Bin Zuhayr (RA)

1) Quality #1
2) Quality #2
3) Attribute or something important about him.

Chapter 5

The Covenant of Medinah

In this chapter, we will study the covenant (pact) the Prophet Muhammad made with the various groups living in Medina and its importance.

The Covenant (Pact) of Medina

The Quraysh considered the safe departure of Prophet Muhammad as a defeat, and they had every intention to take revenge for this defeat on Aws and Khazraj. The Qurayshi leaders, Abu Sufyan and Ubayy bin Khalaf, wrote a letter to the Aws and Khazraj expressing their disappointment over their support for the Prophet Muhammad. The Quraysh asserted they had a rightful claim to Prophet Muhammad as he was one of them, and Aws and Khazraj should remove themselves from this fight.

- Before we get into the details of the pact and its different articles (elements), let's first look at why Prophet Muhammad decided to make this pact with other groups in Medina.

Threats from Quraysh

- Quraysh even threatened the delegation of Aws and Khazraj after they met with the Prophet – they arrested one of their prominent leaders, Saad Bin Ubadah, during this trip to Makkah to intimidate him.
- At that time, the Prophet warned the leaders of Aws and Khazraj about facing an enemy who was more powerful and enjoyed leadership in the region.
- On the other hand, Aws and Khazraj were fully aware of the threats. They were ready to risk their lives, property, and peace to protect the Messenger of God on earth.

The Covenant (Pact) of Medina

- The Prophet realized that if Quraysh attacked Medina, a common strategy to defend it would be necessary. The Covenant of Medinah was written to define the rights and responsibilities of various groups and to outline how to defend Medinah.

- Some historical books refer to this covenant (agreement) as the First Constitution of Medina.

Note: A **covenant** (*Meethaq*) is like an agreement but has more religious significance. The **constitution** of a state is usually a larger document that covers many government-related policies that are not covered in this covenant. Hence, it should be considered a temporary agreement to address a specific situation.

Articles of the Covenant

General articles

- Prophet Muhammad initiated this agreement by acting as the Prophet of Allah on Earth.
- The two main parties were: Muslim migrants from Makkah and Muslims from Medina (the local tribes).
- All people who would later migrate or convert to Islam would automatically be included in this pact.
- The two main parties are considered "one community distinct from all others" or "one soul, two bodies".
- If a dispute arises over this covenant, everyone will turn to Allah and His messenger, and their decision will be final in this matter, and everyone is required to accept it.

Crime and injustice

- Migrants would pay blood money and compensation according to their family traditions and would pay ransom to free their relatives from anyone.
- Similarly, the Muslims of Medina would do the same for their people and relatives. The Muslims of Medina will not be responsible for paying such a large sum to any migrant.
- No group will commit oppression and injustice against anyone, and both parties will rise above all tribal relationships for the safety of all Muslims.
- If a Muslim from either side commits a criminal act of hostility and injustice, the other Muslims will collectively act against him like a state (not individually to settle the score).
- If a Muslim kills another Muslim, the killer will be given punishment according to the law specified by Islam at that time.

Fighting and support

- Maintaining peace and harmony in society will be the ultimate goal of every member.
- No member will give preference to any non-believer over a believer (for example, helping a non-believer attack or kill a believer) – all believers will be united in this matter and support each other.
- Medinah will be considered a sacred city where criminals would not be allowed to prosper – every member should try to build a relationship of trust and protection with other members.

- Whoever fights with one party will be considered a fight with all.
- Whoever would make peace with one party will be making peace with all.
- No one will harbor any person or provide material assistance to the people of Quraysh (non-believers).
- No women from Quraysh will be given safe harbor without their guardians' permission.
- No protection will be given to the supporters of Quraysh.
- If Medinah is attacked, all signatories will support efforts to counter.
- In the event of war with an outside party, no individual will be allowed to declare peace on their own; it will be a collective decision.

Articles related to the Jews of Medinah

- The Jews of Medina were accepted as a group of faithful while remaining steadfast in their religion.
- The Jews will settle disputes and matters according to their laws unless they come to the Muslims for help. Then it will be handled in accordance with this agreement.
- The Jews and Muslims will work together for mutual benefit.
- The Jews will have the same rights as the Muslims of Aws and Khazraj, and their rights will be protected if they remain faithful to the Muslims.
- The Jews will remain protected as part of the tribe to which they belong.
- If Medina is attacked from outside, then they will also assist Muslims in protecting this land.
- If they want to participate in the war from the Muslims' side, they need to seek permission from the Prophet.

Difference of opinion:

Historians differ on whether the main Jewish tribes (Banu Nadheer, Banu Qurayzah, and Banu Qaynuqah) were part of this agreement. First, they considered themselves religious scholars, and it was difficult for them to accept the authority of Prophet Muhammad. Some historians were also unable to find their names in the list of parties in this agreement.

Significance of agreements in Islam

Importance of abiding by agreements

- Many people take their promises and written and unwritten contracts lightly.
- Fulfilling a formal contract is the ultimate form of keeping a promise and is greatly emphasized in Islam.
- Keeping promises or contracts is one way to build trust amongst people – building trust is a gradual process.
- The worst promise or agreement in a contract is the one made with the intention of not fulfilling it – it's considered the worst LIE.
- It is better to hurt someone's feelings on the spot than make a false promise or sign a contract that you know you won't fulfill.

وَأَوْفُوا بِالْعَهْدِ ۖ إِنَّ الْعَهْدَ كَانَ مَسْئُولً

Fulfill your promise/contract because it will be asked about (Bani Israel:34)

Do these sound familiar?
"I will keep the trash outside after dinner!"
"No big deal, I will do it!"
"Just give me a minute, I will vacuum."
"I will be there iA at 6:00 PM."

Significance of the Covenant of Medina

- For the first time, people were united by their faith and a sense of community rather than tribal association.
- It showed the non-Muslims in the area that Islam is a religion that strongly believes in the concept of justice and equality in a society.
- It gave them some independence but, at the same time, bound them to work for causes of mutual benefit.
- It made everyone realize they are now part of a new community, where people may belong to different tribes and religions, but share the goal of creating an environment of mutual respect and benefit.
- It helped reduce Ansar's burden and responsibilities.
- It set out a clear policy to confront any expected/unexpected attack from the Quraysh and protect Medina.
- It gave a strong message to the Quraysh that dealing with Prophet Muhammad through violence is not going to be easy for them now.
- It made the Quraysh realize that, to attack Medinah, they would have to deal with neighboring tribes as well, which are allies of Aws and Khazraj.

Importance of agreement in the sight of God

- In Surah Tawbah, Allah punished those who deliberately rejected Prophet Muhammad as a Messenger. The Prophet was asked to declare all contracts with non-believers null and void.
- However, it is explicitly stated that all contracts agreed upon a time frame must continue until the period is over.
- This shows that even under extreme circumstances, Allah does not like breaking contracts.

Lessons for us

- It is important to note that Muslims were fewer in number in Medina. Still, the Prophet, through his prophetic wisdom, negotiated treaties with other groups to solidify the political strength of Muslims against any aggression from the Quraysh.
- The agreement of Medina showed an example for Muslims of how to interact with other religious and ethnic communities in a way that was mutually beneficial and respectful of other ways of life.

We have unwritten contracts with many of our relationships. Pick a relationship, such as parents, siblings, cousins, or neighbors, and imagine having to write a contract with them. What would the contract look like? Create a table outlining the roles and responsibilities you agree on for each side, such as you and your parents or you and your neighbors, etc.

The Source of Peace

- We all love peace in our lives, and Allah is the source of all peace.
- If we follow the teachings given to us by Allah, we will find peace and tranquility in our lives.
- Praying (Salah) is the best way to remember Allah and gain inner peace.
- The best way to gain external peace in one's life and in society is to love the people around them and fulfill other people's rights.
- When a nation is ruled with justice, it brings peace.
- God's attribute of As-Salam shows us where to turn when we face both internal and external chaos.

Verily, Peace (As-Salam) is among the names of Allah He has placed on the Earth, so spread it among yourselves. (Sahih Al-Bukhari # 989)

هُوَ اللَّهُ الَّذِي لَا إِلَهَ إِلَّا هُوَ الْمَلِكُ الْقُدُّوسُ السَّلَامُ

He is Allah besides whom there is no deity, the Sovereign Lord, the Holy, the Embodiment of Peace. (59:23)

Chapter 6

Establishment of the Muslim Ummah (nation)

In this chapter, we will learn how, after the migration to Medina, this small group laid the foundation for the emergence of a vast Muslim Ummah.

Prophet Ibrahim - Father of the Prophets

- Although we have studied this before at the start of the Seerah course, let's review it because it is important to remind us of the relationship of Prophet Muhammad and his nation with Prophet Ibrahim.

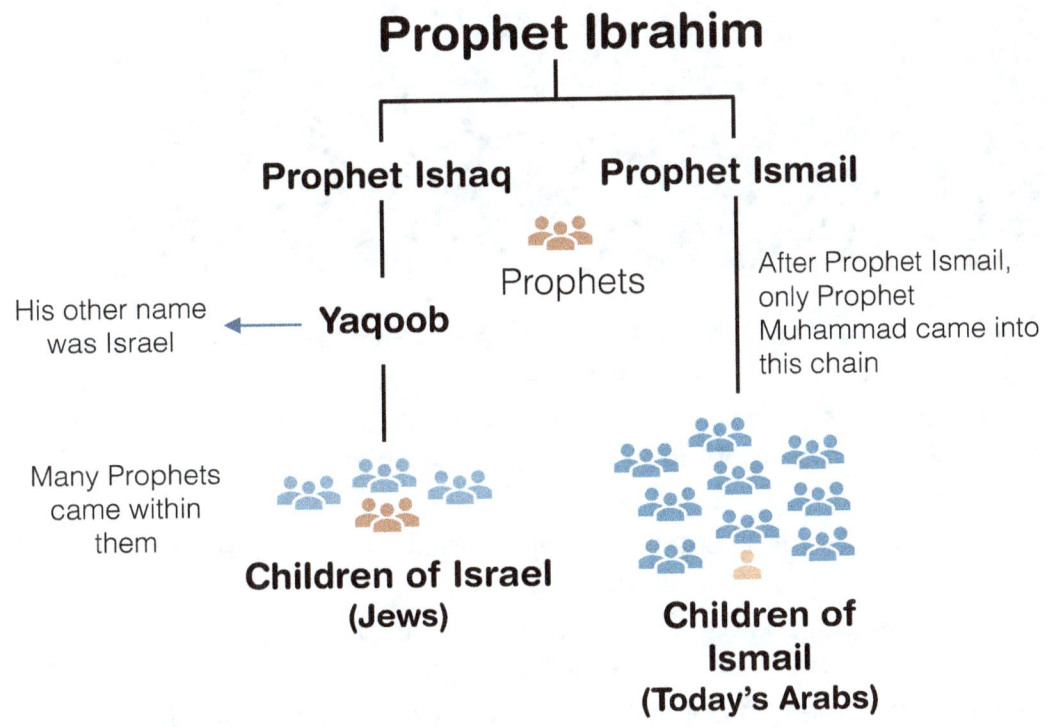

- The history of the children of Prophet Ishaq (Bani Israel) and Ismael (Bani Ismael) should be seen as two parallel nations settled in two different parts of the earth, but governed by the same law of "Divine Justice."
- God chose them to represent His religion and His teachings on earth for any nation unaware of a Prophet's teachings.
- Bani Israel was given the chance first to lead people on earth in their religious guidance. Then it was time for the Children of Ismael to take the lead.
- Both nations were settled in the middle of the earth. Bani Israel was settled in Palestine, and Bani Ismael was settled in the land of Hijaz (today's Saudi Arabia).
- Bani Israel left the path and teachings of their forefather, Prophet Ibrahim.
- Prophet Muhammad and his nation were asked to follow the teachings of Prophet Ibrahim.
- In this chapter, we will see the making of this new nation, the Children of Ismael.

Laws and teachings given to the new nation

Daily prayer and other practices

- Except for a few, most of the practices given to Prophet Muhammad were a revival of those given to Prophet Ibrahim.
- In Medina, the foundation of a new nation (the Muslim Ummah) was laid, which would lead the world and deliver the message of Allah to the surrounding countries.
- For the first time, Muslims could worship collectively in a safe and peaceful environment and implement Allah's instructions.
- Several new instructions were given to develop in Muslims the qualities of character necessary to assume leadership of the world.
- It is reported that the number of times Muslims must pray in a day was finalized when the Prophet had the experience of Mairaj (Ascension). However, it was not a new instruction; all the Prophets before Prophet Muhammad prayed 5 times a day.

Initial Instructions

- Within a few years after the migration, Prophet Muhammad was given initial instructions about:

Community Prayers	Fasting and its details	Revived Hajj and its details
Some concepts of Halal (allowed) and Haram (prohibited)		
Good practices and virtues are appreciated in a society		

Addressing Jews

Children of Israel — **Leadership to guide people in Religion** → **Children of Ismael**

Background

- Before Prophet Muhammad, the Children of Israel (Jews) were the leading Muslim nation.
- The Jews rejected their last Prophet sent to them, who is Jesus. They even tried to kill him, but God saved him.
- They were given the responsibility to preach the religion of God, which has always been Islam, and welcome and accept any new Prophet sent by God.
- That's why Allah reminded both Jews and Christians that they should be the first ones to accept the message of Islam because this is the continuation of the same message.
- In their scriptures, the arrival of Prophet Muhammad has been predicted.
- In Medina, the Jews were a significant political force, and their leaders were influential (because of their knowledge of Torah), so they also became the main addressees of the Quran.
- The main enemies of Islam, who were helping Quraysh in Makkah, were the original Jews, not the Jews who accepted Judaism in Aws and Khazraj.
- Three major Jewish tribes: Banu Nadheer, Banu Qurayzah, and Banu Qaynuqah.
- Up until now, they were only supporting Quraysh, but now there was a fear that they would come in the front as the enemy of Islam.
- God addressed the Jews in the Quran and told them about the shift of leadership. Before giving them this news, He reminded them of all the deviations they have caused in their religion and the reasons for God's decision.

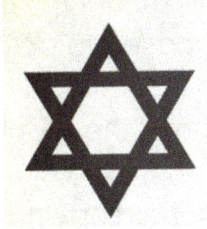 

Misconception of the Jews and Clarifications

Misconceptions of the Jews

- Jews were proud and always felt superior because of the following misconceptions:
    - They are Allah's children and His favorite and beloved group.
    - They have always been worthy of His rewards in this world until the Day of Judgment.
    - A Prophet can NEVER be born outside of the Children of Israel. They were waiting for the last Messenger to come from among them (Bani Israel).
    - They will not be punished in Hell. Even if someone has disobeyed Allah, he/she will be punished for a few days and then sent to Heaven.
- That's why they rejected the message of Islam even after recognizing that Prophet Muhammad was the prophet foretold in their books.
- Before Allah removes them from the leadership position, it was necessary to clarify the position of the Children of Israel and answer all the objections they had raised against the Prophet Muhammad.

Clarification by the Quran – its responsibility not privilege

- When Allah showers His blessings and favor upon a nation, He wants it to be humbled and grateful. It is not a privilege.
- The special status given to a nation is a responsibility of great magnitude.
- Allah gave the Children of Israel the responsibility of focusing on the religion and seeking guidance from it. In return, He will help them against their enemies and allow them to lead the nations around them. This was a kind of agreement between God and the Children of Israel.

Relationship with Prophet Ibrahim

- The Children of Israel (Prophet Moses and Jesus) and Ismail (Prophet Muhammad) were all from the children of Prophet Ibrahim.
- The Jews were invited to get out of their shell and accept Prophet Muhammad, whose roots also go back to Prophet Ibrahim, but they refused.
- As part of the Covenant, the group is supposed to believe in every prophet that is sent to them.
- The Children of Israel did not accept some of the prophets sent to them. They even killed some of them. They can't pick and choose among the prophets.
- When it comes to the Quran, they said they already have a book (the Torah) and that their hearts are 'locked' against hearing anything else.

The birth of the hypocrites – a new enemy

- Since God chided them in the Quran, they resorted to their old techniques.
- Even before Prophet Muhammad, because the Jewish population was very low, they used hidden schemes and other tactics to become dominant in the lands they lived in – the same in Medina.
- First, they made the impression that since the teachings of Islam and Judaism are the same, Jews don't need to accept and follow the Quran and the Prophet.
- Some of the Jews would socialize with Muslims in such a way as if they had already accepted Islam in secret, and they were already part of the Muslim community.
- This created an entire group of people who had the strategy to harm Islam and Muslims from within – the Quran called this group the Hypocrites (Munafiqeen).
- A hypocrite is a person whose intentions and actions do not match, and Allah is aware of them.
- Simple people were impressed by this outward 'sincerity' (but it was a tactic).
- God exposed them in the Quran on many occasions, alerting Prophet Muhammad and Muslims to use caution and be aware of the schemes of these people.

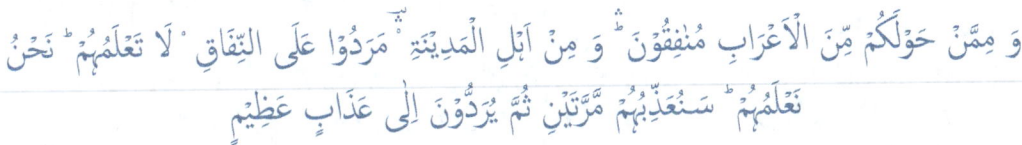

There are also many hypocrites among the Bedouins who live around you, and among the inhabitants of Medina also. They have become adept at their hypocrisy. You do not know them; We know them. Soon, We shall punish them twice. Then they will be pushed towards great torment. (9:101)

Restoration of Qibla for Prayers

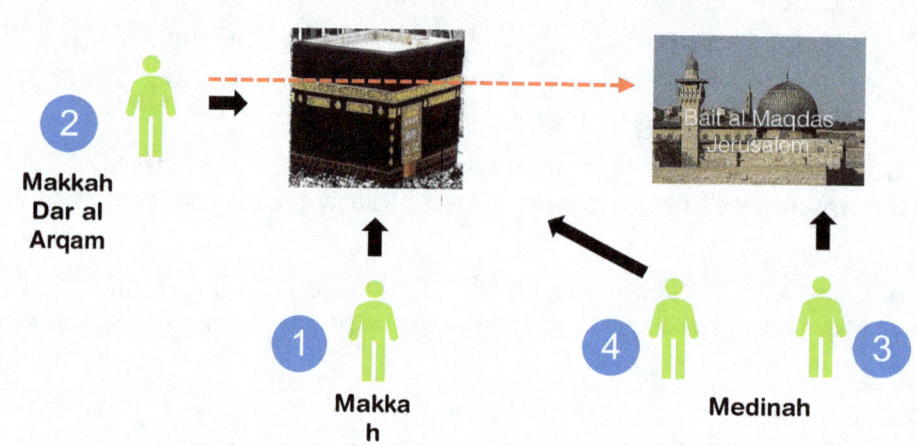

As mentioned earlier, God has a special law for both the Children of Israel and Ismael, to test their faith in this life. This is precisely what happened when it comes to setting the Qibla for prayers in Makkah and Medina.

1. Before prophethood, people in Makkah used to pray facing the Kabaah, following the tradition of Prophet Ibrahim.

2. After prophethood, the Prophet was told to follow the Children of Israel in some matters, including facing Bait al-Maqdis (Palestine) for prayers.
Prophet Muhammad wanted to follow Allah's instructions, but his heart was still attached to the Kabaah. So, he chose Dar al Arqam for prayers, which allowed him to face both the Kabaah and the Bait al Maqdis simultaneously (red arrow).

3. After moving to Medina, the Prophet couldn't face both because of Medina's location.

4. One and a half years after migration, the Prophet was instructed by Allah to face the Kabaah again. The Prophet was in the middle of Dhuhur or Asr prayers at a mosque now known as Masjid Al Qiblatain (the mosque of two Qiblahs) at that time. A companion of the Prophet went out and announced to everyone that the Qiblah had been changed and that everyone should pray facing the Kabaah again.

Qibla = The place or direction one faces to perform religious practices like prayers.

Why the Qiblah was changed twice

When the Qibla for prayers was shifted from the Kabaah to the Bait Al Maqdis.

When the Qibla for prayers was shifted back to the Kabaah.

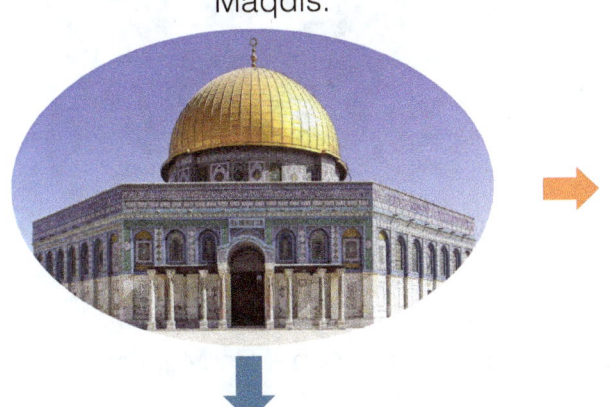

Muslims were **tested** because they had a bond with Kabaah.

New Muslims who were Jews before were **tested** because they had a bond with Bait Al-Maqdis.

Children of Ismail as the Middle Nation

- After the change of the Qibla, the Quran referred to the Children of Ismail, the new religious leaders, the Middle Nation. They will convey the message of Islam from the Prophet to the rest of the world until the Day of Judgment.

- For Muslims to play their role effectively, the Prophet not only recited the Quran to them but also explained it, correcting their actions when he found errors or negligence.

- Muslims living outside Medina were asked to either come live in Medina or spend time there so they could be trained by the Prophet for this major task ahead.

Middle Nation

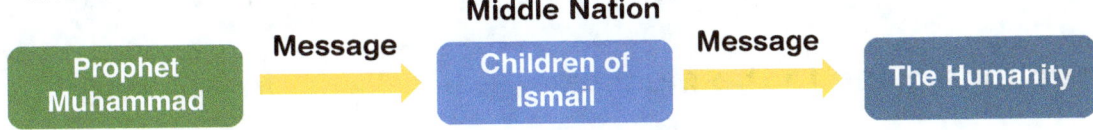

وَ كَذٰلِكَ جَعَلْنٰكُمْ أُمَّةً وَّسَطًا لِّتَكُوْنُوْا شُهَدَآءَ عَلَى النَّاسِ وَ يَكُوْنَ الرَّسُوْلُ عَلَيْكُمْ شَهِيْدًا

"And it is thus that We appointed you (children of Ismail) to be the community of the middle so that you might be witnesses to all mankind and the Messenger might be a witness over you." (2:143)

Permission to fight and its principles

Muslims in Makkah were not allowed to fight with the Quraysh because Islam does not allow fighting within a state or country. Fighting is only allowed (if necessary) between two states or countries, in accordance with the rules of war.

- Jews did not like the change of Qibla at all, while Muslims were taking root in Medina.
- Quraysh's hopes for Muslims' failure in the new environment did not come true.
- Quraysh felt it was necessary to take corrective actions before Muslims started gaining more power in the new land.
- At this moment, the Prophet and his companions were informed by Allah that they were now allowed to fight back.
- Allah gave them clear instructions on:
    - How to seek Allah's help through prayers and perseverance during the war.
    - Responding to the enemy's attack and developing a plan for that.
    - What is allowed and what is not allowed while fighting a war?
- Allah told them that as a result of this permission to fight, Muslims would face issues related to fear, the danger of loss of life and wealth, shortage of food and other supplies, as a test from Allah.

وَ لَنَبْلُوَنَّكُمْ بِشَىْءٍ مِّنَ الْخَوْفِ وَ الْجُوْعِ وَ نَقْصٍ مِّنَ الْاَمْوَالِ وَ الْاَنْفُسِ وَ الثَّمَرٰتِ ۚ وَ بَشِّرِ الصّٰبِرِيْنَ

[In this cause] We shall definitely test you with some fear and famine, loss of life and wealth, and loss in [producing] fruits (other crops). (2:155)

Instructions given to the Muslim

- The instructions for the Muslims are given in Surah Baqarah Verses 190-194.
- If the disbelievers start a war, Muslims are allowed to fight back.
- This battle would be for the sake of Allah and His religion (not for grabbing land or showing strength).
- If the disbelievers declare war during the sacred months (when fighting was not allowed in Arabia), the believers will fight back.

- Muslims will never begin any fight within the boundaries of Haram (the area around Kabaah that is considered sacred), but if the disbelievers start, then Muslims are allowed to fight back.
- Once war is started, the Muslims must continue to fight and punish disbelievers until Islam becomes supreme in the Arabian land, and the strength of the disbelievers to fight is removed completely.
- Once victory is achieved, the disbelievers will be expelled from the land if they stop fighting Muslims. Otherwise, they will be killed, and no asylum will be given to them in Makkah.
- The only choice left with disbelievers is to either accept Islam or be killed.
- Muslims should refrain from committing any excesses.

The fight between Believers and Disbelievers occurred in several stages, which we will cover as we progress.

Why did Allah allow fighting?

- Islam is the religion of Allah, which is closest to human nature and to human beings who seek peace and security at all times.
- Allah has mentioned in many places in the Quran that He does not like chaos and disturbance in a society.
- Under normal circumstances, we are asked to be kind and gentle to spread peace and love in society.

- However, sometimes, war is necessary to gain long-term peace, especially when innocent people are mistreated.
- Allah told us the reason He allows one nation to fight another.

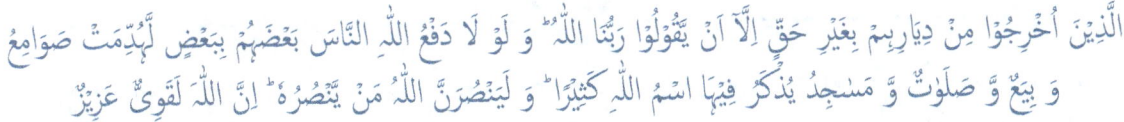

الَّذِينَ أُخْرِجُوا مِنْ دِيَارِهِمْ بِغَيْرِ حَقٍّ إِلَّا أَنْ يَقُولُوا رَبُّنَا اللَّهُ ۗ وَ لَوْ لَا دَفْعُ اللَّهِ النَّاسَ بَعْضَهُمْ بِبَعْضٍ لَّهُدِّمَتْ صَوَامِعُ وَ بِيَعٌ وَّ صَلَوَاتٌ وَّ مَسَاجِدُ يُذْكَرُ فِيهَا اسْمُ اللَّهِ كَثِيرًا ۗ وَ لَيَنْصُرَنَّ اللَّهُ مَنْ يَّنْصُرُهُ ۗ إِنَّ اللَّهَ لَقَوِيٌّ عَزِيزٌ

Those who have been evicted from their homes without any reason - only because they say, "Our Lord is Allah." And were it not that Allah checks the people (through force), some using others, there would have been destroyed monasteries, churches, synagogues, and mosques in which the name of Allah is much mentioned. And Allah will surely support those who support Him. Indeed, Allah is Powerful and Exalted in Might. (Hajj: 40)

Lessons for us

Children of Ismail Today

- The Children of Israel previously served as the Middle Nation for the rest of the world.
- The Children of Ismail (mostly Arabs) are the Middle Nation today, as described in the Quran.
- No other Prophet is going to come, and they are responsible for delivering the message of Islam to other nations.
- Muslims, who are not from the Children of Ismail (non-Arabs), must help them continue this huge task. Their role is primarily that of supporters, but they are indirectly sharing the responsibility.

Fighting Today

- The only reason Muslims were permitted to fight was that it is the law of Allah that He punishes the people who reject a Messenger of Allah among them. Allah told the Prophet that he and his companions would fight a war with the disbelievers and punish them.
- However, it is important to note that Allah did not allow the Prophet and his companions to fight while still living with the disbelievers in Makkah.
- They were first asked to migrate and establish another state.
- Similarly, all other instructions related to the Muslims living in society started coming down after the migration.
- This type of fighting, associated with the Messengers, no longer applies. However, **Muslim nations** must fight against aggressor nations if they have the strength to do so.
- Muslim groups cannot fight other nations in the name of Islam.

1. How do daily and weekly prayers in the mosque help us form a stronger sense of community?
2. What do you suggest we can do to allow the non-Muslims around us to learn about Islam?
3. Wars result in loss of life, safety, peace, wealth, etc. What should nations in the world do to live peacefully together?

The Source of Security

الْمُؤْمِنُ

- Allah calls Himself the Source of Security and Faith.
- By believing in Allah, we achieve the ultimate form of faith and receive security in this world and the Hereafter.
- There is no faith and security better than from the one who is the King of kings and controls everything.
- By believing in one true Allah, we secure ourselves from misguidance and believing in false gods that do not exist and cannot help us in times of need.
- If we want to strengthen our faith, we should ask the Source of all faith, that is, Allah.
- Prophet Muhammad has taught us many duas to say when we feel insecure or are in a state of danger.

هُوَ اللّٰهُ الَّذِىْ لَآ اِلٰهَ اِلَّا هُوَ ۚ اَلْمَلِكُ الْقُدُّوْسُ السَّلٰمُ الْمُؤْمِنُ الْمُهَيْمِنُ الْعَزِيْزُ الْجَبَّارُ الْمُتَكَبِّرُ ۚ سُبْحٰنَ اللّٰهِ عَمَّا يُشْرِكُوْنَ

He is the very God besides whom there is no deity, the Sovereign Lord, the Holy, the Embodiment of Peace, the Giver of Peace (tranquility), the Guardian, the Mighty, the Extremely Powerful, the Most High; exalted is God above what they state as partners! (59:23)

MY GLOBAL MUSLIM FAMILY

1. Afghanistan
2. Indonesia
3. Turkey
4. Sudan
5. Iraq
6. Morocco
7. Malaysia
8. Tunisia
9. Maldives
10. Egypt

Instructions

1. Print the world map on paper. You can also print only the part of the world where Muslim countries are located.
2. Pick three countries from the list above.
3. Mark them on the map using thumbtacks.
4. Collect five interesting facts about those three countries and write them on paper.

Chapter 7

Battle of Badr

In this chapter, we will learn about the most decisive battle in the history of Islam, which was not a regular battle but a punishment for the disbelievers.

Quiz

Do you know what **Jihad** is, and what you have heard about it, positive or negative?

Concept of Jihad

- We learned in the previous chapter that God allowed Muslims to fight Jihad, but let's understand this word and the concept associated with it.
- Two terms are used interchangeably for fighting, but they differ when used in specific contexts.

Jihad

Strive or struggle. The Quran also uses the word for fighting, but it generally means any struggle for something. For example, studying hard can also be Jihad. Helping others can be a Jihad.

Qitaal

This word is used specifically in the context of fighting. Qitaal and Jihad are sometimes used interchangeably, but when Qitaal is used, it means fighting.

- Jihad is generally used when we make an effort for the sake of God. Any good deed can be done for the sake of God, including studying hard to pass the exams.
- Jihad/Qitaal in the context of fighting is allowed to the Messengers of Allah when Allah commands them to punish the disbelievers after they reject the message – this type of Jihad is specific to the Messengers of Allah.
- When Messenger is present, participating in the Jihad can be optional or mandatory.
- The Messengers cannot take up arms in the fight until Allah permits them; however, when the mandatory call for Jihad is made, then not participating in it becomes a grave sin.
- After the time of the Messengers, Jihad/Qitaal can only be done against the oppression of fundamental human rights.
- Jihad/Qitaal can only be declared by a Muslim country against another country, following the rules of engagement – there is no concept of Jihad within a country between groups.

Battle of Badr

Steps taken to protect Medinah

- The Prophet regularly sent informers throughout Medina to monitor attacks from outside.
- Jews were settled around Medina, so he signed a separate agreement with the Jewish tribes of Banu Nadheer, Banu Qurayzah, and Banu Qaynuqah, under which they agreed not to allow any attacks from outside.

- He also made agreements with many tribes settled along the route between Makkah and Medinah to secure their support, or at least their neutrality in this fight.
- All these arrangements were made so the Quraysh would know that Muslims are ready for any surprise attack.
- The Prophet also sent armed groups of companions on various routes towards Medina. Those armed missions are called Sariyyah.

The background and reasons

- A massive Quraysh trade caravan led by Abu Sufyan was coming from Syria and heading towards Makkah.
- A minor incident had already occurred between Muslims and the caravan, which made Abu Sufyan assume that on the way to Makkah, Muslims from Medinah would attack them. So they asked Quraysh to send help from Makkah.
- The leaders of Quraysh decided that, under the garb of protecting the trade caravan, they should go with full force and eliminate Muslims once and for all.
- They considered it a golden opportunity to kill the Prophet.
- On the other hand, the Prophet saw both groups (the caravan and the Quraish coming to fight) in a dream. Allah commanded the Prophet to prepare his men to fight the Quraysh.
- The Prophet was not aware at that time which group his men would meet.
- When Muslims reached near Badr, they learned from their informants that the trade caravan had left the area and was already heading towards Makkah. This means there was no possibility of them meeting the caravan.
- They soon realized that the group that Allah wanted them to fight was the army of Quraysh, not the caravan.

The Place of Badr

Group A: A Quraysh trade caravan coming from Syria, heading towards Makkah

1

Caravan

Syria

Safely arrived in Makkah

N

Muslims Army

3 Prophet saw a dream for one of the two groups

Badr

Medina

Quraysh

Makkah

2 **Group B:** The leaders of Quraysh are coming with a whole army

From the direction that Muslims took, it was clear that they wanted to meet the Quraish army, not the caravan.

The first battle between Truth and falsehood

The Quran states the punishment for the Quraysh:

Fight them; God will **punish them through your hands** and will humiliate them and grant you dominance through His help (Tauba:14)

- The first battle that occurred between the believers and Quraysh was the Battle of Badr – which took place in the 2nd Hijrah (more than one year after the migration) at the location of Badr.
- It is not considered an ordinary battle in the history of Islam, but a clash between the forces of Truth and falsehood.
- Allah wanted to punish the disbelievers who not only forced the Messenger and his companions from their homeland but also did everything to humiliate and harm him.
- All the indications from the Quran and authentic Seerah are that the battle was 'staged' by Allah to punish Quraysh's top leadership.
- As Allah said in the Quran, they have plans, and He has plans, and He is the best planner.
- The complete destruction of the Quraysh was not in Allah's scheme, but He wanted to break their leadership.

Removing a Misconception

Some historians reported that Muslims wanted to rob the trade caravan, but accidentally got into a fight with the Quraysh.

- If Muslims had wanted to attack the trade caravan, they should have headed north of Medina rather than southwest (as shown in the picture above).
- It is reported that on the way, Quraysh heard the news that the trade caravan of Abu Sufyan had already safely left the route, which Muslims could have attacked; then why did they continue towards Badr?
- If Quraysh intended to protect the trade caravan, one might ask why they brought a fully equipped army of 1,000 and marched toward Medina.
- Quraysh announced in Makkah that no leader or important person should stay behind and must leave for this mission.
- When Muslims were leaving Medina, the Prophet made this dua: "O Allah, if You allowed Quraysh to destroy this group of people of Islam, there would be no one left to worship You on this earth."

A test for the believers

- The Prophet told his companions about his dream, and he was promised victory over one group – his actions suggest he hoped to meet the army of Quraysh.

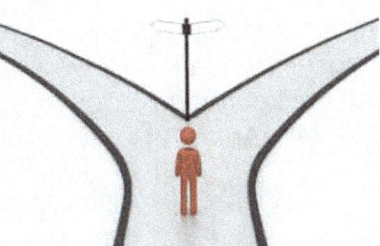

- This became a test in the ranks of the believers – few were unwilling to deal with the army and wanted to take on the Caravan.
- He asked many of his companions about the situation, and most expressed their commitment to fighting the enemy.

Quran and Ahadith about Battle of Badr

كَمَآ أَخْرَجَكَ رَبُّكَ مِنْ بَيْتِكَ بِالْحَقِّ وَ إِنَّ فَرِيقًا مِّنَ الْمُؤْمِنِينَ لَكَرِهُونَ

يُجَادِلُونَكَ فِى الْحَقِّ بَعْدَ مَا تَبَيَّنَ كَأَنَّمَا يُسَاقُونَ إِلَى الْمَوْتِ وَ هُمْ يَنْظُرُونَ

"[It is] just as when your Lord brought you out of your home [for the battle of Badr] in truth, while indeed, a party among the believers was unwilling, arguing with you concerning the truth after it had become clear as if they were being driven toward death while they were looking on." (Anfal:5-6)

إِذْ أَنتُم بِالْعُدْوَةِ الدُّنْيَا وَ هُم بِالْعُدْوَةِ الْقُصْوَى وَ الرَّكْبُ أَسْفَلَ مِنكُمْ وَ لَوْ تَوَاعَدتُّمْ لَاخْتَلَفْتُمْ فِى الْمِيعَادِ وَ

لَٰكِن لِّيَقْضِىَ اللَّهُ أَمْرًا كَانَ مَفْعُولًا لِّيَهْلِكَ مَنْ هَلَكَ عَنْ بَيِّنَةٍ وَ يَحْيَى مَنْ حَىَّ عَنْ بَيِّنَةٍ وَ إِنَّ اللَّهَ لَسَمِيعٌ

"[Remember] when you were on the near side of the valley, and they (Quraysh) were on the farther side, and the trade caravan was lower [in position] than you. Even if you had made an appointment [to meet], you would have missed it, [but Allah did not miss it]. But [it was] so that Allah might accomplish a matter already destined – that those who were destined to perish [through disbelief] would perish upon evidence and those who lived [in faith] would live upon evidence; and indeed, Allah is Hearing and Knowing." (Anfal:42)

إِذْ تَسْتَغِيثُونَ رَبَّكُمْ فَاسْتَجَابَ لَكُمْ أَنِّى مُمِدُّكُم بِأَلْفٍ مِّنَ الْمَلَٰئِكَةِ مُرْدِفِينَ

[Remember] when you asked for help from your Lord, and He answered you, 'Indeed, I will reinforce/help you with a thousand from the angels, following one another.'" [Quran, Anfal:9]

إِذْ يُوحِى رَبُّكَ إِلَى الْمَلَٰئِكَةِ أَنِّى مَعَكُمْ فَثَبِّتُوا الَّذِينَ ءَامَنُوا سَأُلْقِى فِى قُلُوبِ الَّذِينَ كَفَرُوا الرُّعْبَ

فَاضْرِبُوا فَوْقَ الْأَعْنَاقِ وَاضْرِبُوا مِنْهُمْ كُلَّ بَنَانٍ

"[Remember] when your Lord inspired to the angels, 'I am with you, so strengthen those who have believed. I will cast terror into the hearts of those who disbelieved, so strike [them] upon the necks and strike them on every part of their body.'" [Quran, Anfal:12]

"O Prophet of Allah! Do what Allah has instructed you to. We are with you in every situation. By Allah! We will not give the answer that the Israelites gave to Musa, 'You and your Lord go and fight; we are sitting here." (Hadith)

"We have believed in your prophethood. We are witnesses that what you have brought is true. We have promised to obey you; do what we should do. We are with you. We swear by Allah if you ask us to enter into the sea, we will jump into it, and not one will remain behind." (Hadith)

Some facts about the Battle

Number of people in Quraysh's Army

1000+

Number of people in Muslim Army

313

Entire leadership of Quraysh participated in the Battle

The Prophet **consulted his companions** and changed his key strategies few times when preparing for the battle.

Allah promised the Prophet that **1000 angels** will be fighting with the Muslims.

The night before the battle, **Allah put the believers to deep sleep**, and they felt refreshed next morning.

The ground was sandy, and it was hard to keep their feet firm. **Allah sent down rain**, which settled the sand and gave them a pit of water to drink from.

Disbelievers killed = **70**

Believers martyred = **14**

Disbelievers captured = **70**

Allah made the army of **Quraysh look small in number** to the Muslims to take away the fear of a large army.

Muslims won this battle with clear victory, and most of the **top leaders of the Quraysh leadership were perished.**

Quran called it the "Day of Furqan"

- The Quran calls the day of the Battle of Badr the Day of Furqan (the Day that separates truth from falsehood).
- Allah wanted to destroy and kill the top leadership of Quraysh as a punishment for rejecting a messenger and humiliating him.
- He promised the Prophet that angels would fight alongside the Muslims.
- This battle broke the back of Quraysh's leadership, and their downfall started.
- On this day, Allah told Muslims in clear terms that if they help Allah's religion, support the Messenger, and act righteously, Allah will help them and make them leaders of this world, but it's a long journey, and a lot of patience is required.
- When the news was given to the Prophet that all frontline leaders of the Quraysh had been killed, he prayed two rakah of Salah and thanked Allah for His support and for fulfilling His promise.

The Prisoners of War

- Seventy men of the Quraysh were taken prisoner.
- Allah clearly told Muslims in the Quran (Surah Muhammad) that 'taking people as slaves from the war is not allowed anymore, and they either should be freed as a favor or in exchange for a ransom'.
- Before this battle, prisoners of war used to become slaves. The Quran terminated the practice of taking new slaves.
- This was the first step towards reducing slave practices.
- Allah also told Muslims that the main objective is to punish them and not take them as prisoners of war.
- The Prophet took a maximum of 4,000 dirhams and a minimum of 1,000 dirhams per person, depending on their family's situation.
- Some were asked to teach Muslim children how to read and write. Some were released on the promise of remaining neutral and not harming Muslims.
- Allah and His Messenger reminded the prisoners of war and the Quraysh that the responsibility of the war, defeat, and the humiliation of paying ransom falls on Quraysh's behavior and their enmity towards the Messenger – they should look at it as a great punishment descended upon them, and they still have the opportunity to mend their ways.

The Muslims of Badr

وَعَدَ اللّٰهُ الَّذِينَ اٰمَنُوْا مِنْكُمْ وَ عَمِلُوا الصّٰلِحٰتِ لَيَسْتَخْلِفَنَّهُمْ فِى الْاَرْضِ كَمَا اسْتَخْلَفَ الَّذِينَ مِنْ قَبْلِهِمْ ۖ وَ لَيُمَكِّنَنَّ لَهُمْ دِيْنَهُمُ الَّذِى ارْتَضٰى لَهُمْ وَ لَيُبَدِّلَنَّهُمْ مِّنْ بَعْدِ خَوْفِهِمْ اَمْنًا ۚ يَعْبُدُوْنَنِىْ لَا يُشْرِكُوْنَ بِىْ شَيْئًا ۚ وَ مَنْ كَفَرَ بَعْدَ ذٰلِكَ فَاُولٰٓئِكَ هُمُ الْفٰسِقُوْنَ

Allah has promised to those of you who believe and do good that He will most certainly give them authority on the earth as He gave authority to those before them and that He will most certainly establish for them their religion which He has chosen for them, and that He will most certainly, after their fear, give them security in exchange; they shall serve Me, not associating anything with Me; and whoever is ungrateful after this, these it is who are the transgressors. (Surah Noor: 55)

Angel Jibrael came to the Prophet and said, "How do you look upon the warriors of Badr among yourselves?" The Prophet said, "As the best of the Muslims." On that, Jibrael said, "And so are the Angels who participated in the Badr (battle)." [Sahih Al-Bukhari]

Graves of the Martyrs of Badr

Reaction of Quraysh in Makkah

- The people surrounded the first person to return to Makkah – they were all anticipating good news.
- They were in shock that most of the leadership of Quraysh was dead.
- Safwan Bin Umayyah suggested checking whether this person has become crazy, and that his sanity be authenticated.
- Abu Lahab did not go to the war because he was predicted to be destroyed in the Quran (Surah Lahab), and he was afraid. He asked his surviving nephew about the war, and he informed: "We came face to face, and the next thing we knew, we bent our heads. They struck on necks as they wished and made us captives as they wished."
- Abu Lahab sent another person to his place to avoid war, but he could not save himself from the punishment of Allah. Just a few days after the battle, he contracted smallpox and died in solitude, as no relative wanted to come near him.
- The entire Makkah went into mourning over this significant loss of leadership.

Summary

- The Battle of Badr is a unique event in the history of Islam because it was not an ordinary battle between two armies.
- The Battle of Badr was an important moment in the struggle between Islam and disbelief that had begun 15 years prior in Makkah.
- Allah planned that battle to punish the disbelievers so people around them could witness the truth that the Prophet brought.
- People often ask about the physical evidence of the claim that Prophet Muhammad was the true messenger of Allah.
- The Battle of Badr is a physical event recorded in the Quran for people to witness until the Day of Judgment.

What things were different in the Battle of Badr that we cannot apply today if Muslims were to fight non-Muslims in a battle?

The Irresistible Subduer

- This is one of the names of Allah that shows His capability to overpower and overwhelm every creation.
- No matter what, He is always dominant over everything.
- The name "Al Qahir" also appeared in the Quran and has a similar meaning.
- Sometimes, we may see that human beings are in control (and we do not see any role of Allah), but in reality, Allah allowed this to happen for a reason.
- Quraysh thought that they were in command. They will do every bad thing possible to the Muslims, expel them from their city, bring an army of 1000 soldiers to kill them, and in the end, they will be dominant.
- Allah showed in the Battle of Badr that He is the Ultimate Irresistible Subduer by sending Angels to help the Muslims.

يَوْمَ تُبَدَّلُ الْأَرْضُ غَيْرَ الْأَرْضِ وَ السَّمٰوٰتُ وَ بَرَزُوْا لِلّٰهِ الْوَاحِدِ الْقَهَّارِ

Remember the day when this earth will be replaced by another and this sky too, and everyone [alone and helpless] will set off towards God, the One and Irresistible Subduer. (14:48)

SEERAH ACTIVITY

Time to Complete: _____

Instructions: Please print this page and complete it or fill it out here.

WORD MATCH

Write the most suitable and related word or letter in front of each statement.

1. Fighting in the path of Allah – [   ]
2. The Quran called the Day of the Battle of Badr – [   ]
3. Number of people in the Muslim army – [   ]
4. They fought with the Muslims in the battle – [   ]
5. The Quraish trade caravan was coming from – [   ]
6. The Prophet saw before the battle – [   ]
7. The Battle of Badr was this from Allah for Quraish – [   ]
8. In the Battle of Badr, all of them got killed – [   ]
9. The Muslim Army captured them – [   ]
10. This war was the first step in stopping it – [   ]

A. Angels   B. Slavery   C. Quraish Leaders   D. 313

E. Punishment   F. Jihad/Qitaal   G. Prisoners of War

H. Al-Furqan   I. Dream   J. Syria

Chapter 8

Onslaught by the enemies of Islam

In this chapter, we will learn the reaction of Quraish, Makkan, and Jews when they suffered a humiliating defeat at the hands of Muslims supported by God and the Angel.

Victory of the Byzantian Romans

- Recall that at the time of the first migration of Muslims to Abyssinia, the Persians defeated the Romans, and, due to Christian support from Abyssinia, the Quraish were joyful at the Romans' defeat.
- Interestingly, the Quran discussed this incident in Surah Rum and then predicted that the Romans would win back.
- Right at the moment when Muslims defeated Quraish in the Battle of Badr, the Romans defeated the Persians as predicted by the Quran.

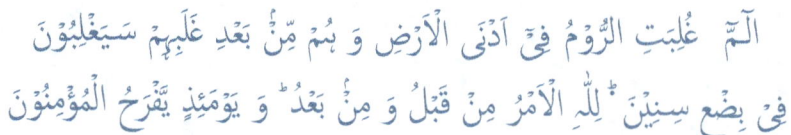

This is Surah Alif Lam Meem. The Byzantines have been defeated in the nearest land. But after their defeat, they will overcome within **three to nine years**. To God belongs the command before and after, and on that day, the believers will rejoice in the victory of God (Surah Rum: 1-4)

- This is one of the most explicit prophecies (divine predictions) in the whole Quran. God ended the verse by saying that "on that day, the believers will rejoice in the victory of God." This also indicates the victory in the Battle of Badr.
- When this Surah was revealed, one of the leaders of the Quraish, Ubay ibn Khalaf, mocked Abu Bakr, saying, "Do you really think the Romans will beat the Persians after this vicious defeat?" Abu Bakr said, "Yes, of course." This showed Abu Bakr's faith in the Prophet Muhammad, as he was telling them what the Quran revealed.
- Ubay died in the Battle of Badr, and he could not see the prediction of the Quran unfold in front of his eyes.

Predictions

- The divine predictions (news about the future) are also called prophecies, and the Quran has made a few.
- We just learned about the Byzantine Romans' victory. Some others were: the conquest of Makkah, the death of Abu Lahab, the Preservation of the original text of the Quran, the coming of the children of Gog and Magog in the end times, and taking over the world, etc.

Fighting on multiple fronts after Badr

Muslims were facing many enemies

- The Core Muslims who were sincere with Islam were facing various open and hidden enemies.

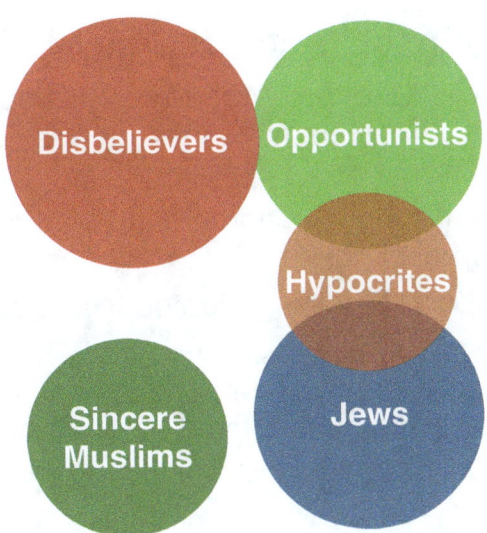

- The group of hypocrites was led by Abdullah Bin Ubayy and comprised of people from Aws and Khazraj, especially those who accepted Judaism, and some from among the Children of Israel, and they were backed by the larger group of the Jews controlled by the Rabbis.

The plot to kill the Prophet

- The young men of Quraysh were extremely frustrated by the killing of most of their leaders.
- Safwan bin Umayyah convinced Umair bin Wahab to travel to Medina and kill the Prophet.
- In compensation, he promised to pay off all his debts and also take care of his children.
- Umair dipped his sword in poison and left for Medinah, where Omar stopped him at the door of the Prophet's mosque.
- He tried to make an excuse, but the Prophet told him the real reason for his trip and informed him of the conversation Safwan had with him.

- Umair got shocked because he knew that no one was aware of this conversation unless Allah told the Prophet about it.
- He realized his mistake and accepted Islam.
- Safwan kept waiting for Umair to bring the good news, but the Prophet won Umair's loyalty.

The impact of victory in the Battle of Badr (Opportunists)

- The victory in the Battle of Badr established beyond doubt that the Muslims are now a real political entity. They are no longer the weak group whom Quraish used to persecute.
- This caused a significant change in and around Medina, and a slight change in Makkah in people's approach towards Islam.
- Many people in and around Medina accepted Islam, seeing the increasing strength of Muslims.
- They wanted to make sure that when Muslims gained power and became financially stronger, they were not deprived of the benefits.
- Some Jews adopted a policy of 'friendly relationship' while keeping hostility in their hearts.
- Some sincere Jews accepted Islam as a result of seeing that Allah delivered His promise of punishing the disbelievers from Quraysh.
- Many new Muslims were not sincere in Islam, and they joined the ranks of hypocrites
- The remaining leaders of Quraysh and most of the Jews now started considering Muslims as a serious threat to their survival.
- They planned to attack Islam from various fronts to keep them busy.

Is it OK to accept something and join a group of people, especially in matters of religion, just because it has more influence and is powerful?

The Role of Jews & Hypocrites

The betrayal of Banu Qaynuqah

- Some Jewish tribes were still sympathetic towards Quraysh, but the Quran exposed their satanic role.
- The Prophet went to their community and reminded them of their promise and contract, and warned them of the same fate as Quraysh.
- The Jews rudely responded to the Prophet: "O Muhammad, you consider us under your rule. Please do not make the mistake of fighting us because previously, you fought a nation that did not know how to wage war. You caused harm to them, but if you fight us, you will find out what the real fighters are like."
- Prophet Muhammad was aware that Banu Qaynuqah had already breached their contract, but he took no action. However, after they attacked a Muslim woman, which resulted in the death of one of their men and one Muslim, the Prophet surrounded them with his army.
- Their leader (also the leader of the hypocrites) requested that Prophet Muhammad spare their lives. The Prophet agreed but asked Banu Qaynuqah to leave the surroundings of Medina, as he was expecting that they would continue to harm Muslims.
- They migrated to Syria, and the Prophet renewed the contract with the remaining two tribes.

Attitude of the Hypocrites

- The hypocrites are discussed in the Quran in many places, as they were causing more harm to the Muslims than any other group, especially to the weaker Muslims. The Quran exposed them.

- Abdullah bin Ubayy was considered their chief (as Allah informed the Prophet). He accepted Islam to destroy Muslims from within.
- Why was he against the Prophet? Some leaders of Aws and Khazraj wanted to make him their chief just before they chose Prophet Muhammad as their leader.
- As a result, Abdullah harbored a personal grudge against the Prophet.

- They used to consider every achievement a result of their intelligence and try to convince others that 'relying on Allah and His promises is a dangerous act'.
- Being Muslims, they had easy access to the Prophet and all the collective decisions that Muslims were taking.
- They used these opportunities to create doubts about the future of Islam and raise objections to the Quran and the Prophets.

Prophet Muhammad is reported to have said about them: "Among the signs of these hypocrites are three, even if he fasts and prays and claims to be a Muslim: when he speaks, he lies, when he gives a promise, he breaks it, and when he is trusted, he betrays." (Sahih Muslim #59)

- Prophet Muhammad and Muslims were unaware of them, but God informed them.

وَ مِمَّنْ حَوْلَكُمْ مِّنَ الْأَعْرَابِ مُنْفِقُوْنَ ۚ وَ مِنْ اَهْلِ الْمَدِيْنَةِ ۛ مَرَدُوْا عَلَى النِّفَاقِ ۚ لَا تَعْلَمُهُمْ ۭ نَحْنُ نَعْلَمُهُمْ

There are also many hypocrites among the Bedouins who live around you, and among the inhabitants of Medina also. They have become adept at their hypocrisy. You do not know them; We know them. (9:101)

How Prophet dealt with the hypocrites

- The Prophet was a kindhearted man, so even after he knew about their hypocrisy, he continued to deal with them gently.
- The Prophet used to consult them on various matters, and that softness led them to believe that this deceit was bearing fruit.

Muslim Groups

- Some continued to remain soft with them, thinking that this relationship would ultimately bring them into Islam with sincerity.
- The others started hating them and thought a hard attitude was needed to fix their behavior.

فَمَا لَكُمْ فِى الْمُنٰفِقِيْنَ فِئَتَيْنِ وَ اللّٰهُ اَرْكَسَهُمْ بِمَا كَسَبُوْا ۖ اَتُرِيْدُوْنَ اَنْ تَهْدُوْا مَنْ اَضَلَّ اللّٰهُ ۖ وَ مَنْ يُّضْلِلِ اللّٰهُ فَلَنْ تَجِدَ لَهٗ سَبِيْلًا

Then what is the matter with you that you are divided into two groups regarding these Hypocrites? God has turned them back because of what they did. Do you want to guide those whom God [according to His law] has led astray? (4:88)

Quran's advice to the hypocrites

- Not all hypocrites were the same. They were advised according to the reasons behind their hypocrisy.
- Allah revealed large sections of the Quran to advise the weak Muslims (including hypocrites) and told them:
  - First and foremost, enter into Islam with full submission and accept Prophet Muhammad as their sole judge in all their matters.
  - The tests and trials they face are temporary, meant to separate insincere people from sincere ones; a permanent reward from Allah awaits them.
  - Be aware of the negative propaganda from the leaders of the hypocrites, as they are not sincere.
  - Allah does not allow their Messengers to be defeated. Siding with the enemies will cause them to see the same fate as the disbelievers.
  - Their behavior is like that of the disbelievers, so even if they escape the punishment in this world, they will be thrown into the lower levels of the Hellfire because of their double game.
  - The only way to correct the behavior is to refrain from opposing Allah and His Messenger and remain sincere with them.
  - Avoid gatherings where the Quran and the Prophet are ridiculed.
  - Avoid gatherings where people conspire against the Prophet.
  - Participate in positive, righteous activities.

يَٰٓأَيُّهَا الَّذِينَ ءَامَنُوا ادْخُلُوا فِى السِّلْمِ كَآفَّةً وَ لَا تَتَّبِعُوا خُطُوَٰتِ الشَّيْطَٰنِ إِنَّهُ لَكُمْ عَدُوٌّ مُّبِينٌ

فَإِنْ زَلَلْتُمْ مِّنْ بَعْدِ مَا جَآءَتْكُمُ الْبَيِّنَٰتُ فَاعْلَمُوا أَنَّ اللَّهَ عَزِيزٌ حَكِيمٌ

Believers! [These two diverse attitudes cannot persist along with faith; so,] enter all of you into God's submission [with one attitude] and do not follow in Satan's footsteps; he is your inveterate foe. If you lapse even after these open warnings, you should know that God is Mighty and very Wise. (2:209)

فَلَا وَ رَبِّكَ لَا يُؤْمِنُونَ حَتَّىٰ يُحَكِّمُوكَ فِيمَا شَجَرَ بَيْنَهُمْ ثُمَّ لَا يَجِدُوا فِىٓ أَنْفُسِهِمْ حَرَجًا مِّمَّا

قَضَيْتَ وَ يُسَلِّمُوا تَسْلِيمًا

But no, [O Messenger!] By your Lord! These people shall never be true believers until they accept you as the arbitrator in their disputes. Then whatever decision you give, they do not feel any uneasiness in their hearts and wholeheartedly submit to it. (4:65)

Muslims were asked to migrate to Medina

- Many tribes outside of Medina accepted the call of Islam.
- The danger in and around Medina was increasing.
- The Prophet sent messages out to these tribes to migrate to Medina to strengthen Islam and Muslims.
- Some people answered the call and moved to Medina, even leaving their family members who did not accept Islam.
- Some did not because, although they accepted Islam, they did not want to get involved in any of the collective issues that Muslims were facing, especially in the light of the struggle going on between Muslims and other groups.
- In the Quran, at one point in this struggle, moving to Medina was considered a sign of true faith.

A gem from the Prophet's morals

When Prophet Muhammad wanted to highlight a mistake (or something he felt was bad behavior) displayed by one of the hypocrites, he would never name the person in front of everyone. He would rather phrase the sentences like this: "What has happened to the people that they are doing such and such an act?" He did that so the person would not feel humiliated in front of other people.

The Repeatedly Forgiving

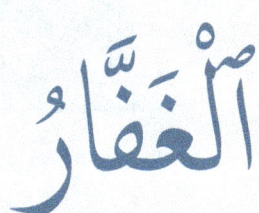

- Al-Ghaffar is the one who accepts our repentance, forgives our faults, covers our mistakes and their effect in this world and the Hereafter.
- The other names of Allah that are similar are Al-Ghafoor and Al-Ghaafir.
- Allah is ready to forgive us at any time, as long as we sincerely repent and make a commitment not to repeat that bad action.
- Allah is so Merciful that He seeks opportunities to forgive us, but we must initiate it.
- When we say Astaghfirullah, we ask for His forgiveness because He is Al-Ghaffar.
- Allah has asked us not to feel depressed or rejected, even if we have committed evil deeds as big as mountains. He wants us to come back to Him and ask for forgiveness.

وَ اِنِّیْ لَغَفَّارٌ لِّمَنْ تَابَ وَ أَمَنَ وَ عَمِلَ صَالِحًا ثُمَّ اهْتَدٰی

However, those who repent, accept faith and do good deeds, then adhere to guidance, for them I am very Forgiving." (20:82)

- Suppose you notice that one of your best friends is experiencing an issue that requires attention. What steps would you take to let him/her know about it and convince him/her to stop?
- Are you sacrificing something for the sake of Allah? Give an example from your daily life where you are sacrificing something to follow the commands of Allah.

Chapter 9

Battle of Uhud

In this chapter, we will learn about the Battle of Uhud, another significant clash between believers and disbelievers, with a slightly different outcome intended by God.

The background of the Battle of Uhud

- The Makkans began planning for the Battle of Uhud immediately after the Battle of Badr. The loss and humiliation of the Battle of Badr were the immediate cause of the Battle of Uhud. Unlike Badr, however, Uhud was the first full-out planned war.

Guarding the Highways of Najd

- After the Battle of Badr, Quraysh sought an alternate route for trade to Syria via Najd.
- Geographically, Medina intersects the caravans that go from Makkah to Syria, and Muslims intercepted and blocked off all routes to Syria.
- Effectively, Quraish cannot trade with Syria anymore, and this would literally destroy their economy. The Makkan economy was based on these supply routes.
- The Quraysh controlled that economy and profited greatly from it. And if you cut off one side of the pipeline, the other side won't function. So, they were in a desperate situation.

An Interesting Incident

- One time, when Muslims were in Najd after hearing news that two tribes wanted to attack them, it started to rain. After the rain had passed, the Prophet took off his shirt, hung it on a tree to dry, and lay down under it to rest.
- A disbeliever approached him quietly and asked while pointing his sword at him: "Who would save you from me today?"
- The Prophet answered: "Allah!" The attacker suddenly froze in terror, and his sword fell from his hand.
- The Prophet picked up the sword and asked him, "Who would save you from me now?" The attacker could not believe that the sword had fallen from his hand, and there was no one to save him from the hands of Prophet Muhammad. The Prophet allowed him to go. He was so impressed by the Prophet's bravery, confidence in Allah, and forgiveness that he accepted Islam immediately and became a Muslim.

Battle of Uhud – A test for the believers

Preparation to attack Medinah

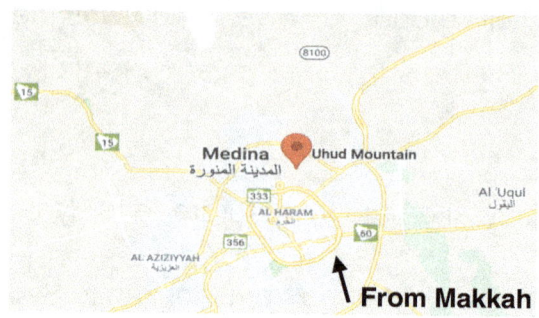

- Quraysh realized that their strength would be insufficient to defeat the Muslims.
- Abu Uzzah was one of the prisoners of the War of Badr. He was released on the condition that he would never fight Muslims, but Safwan bin Umayyah convinced him to go to different tribes and invite them to cooperate.
- Another person was sent to Banu Kananah, and both successfully enlisted support from these tribes.
- An army of around 3,000 people, including 700 armored personnel and 200 mounted troops, marched towards Medina. They also brought widows and children of those who were killed in Badr to motivate the fighters.
- The Muslim guards who used to watch the different highways from Makkah informed Prophet Muhammad of the enemies' march toward Medina.
- The Quraysh's army descended upon Dhul Halifah (outside Medina, where Mount Uhud is) and found the Muslim army standing there, waiting for them.

The dream of the Prophet

- Prophet Muhammad saw a dream that suggested that this fight would be much more challenging than at Badr, but Muslims would still be victorious. He saw a sword that had a jag (a tooth) at its edge (that kind of sword is considered bad), meaning that the Prophet might also get hurt in this battle.
- The Prophet consulted his companions, and some suggested they remain in Medina and fight from there, while others suggested they leave Medina and stop them outside the city. Abdullah bin Ubayy, the leader of the hypocrites, suggested fighting while staying in Medina.
- The suggestion of the sincere companions was: "O Prophet of God! Take us towards the enemy. If we remain in the city, that will be considered a weakness, and the enemy will be encouraged. We have been looking forward to another day when we can meet the enemies of Islam, and God has brought them closer to us."

Marching towards Uhud

- All the sincere companions showed their commitment to the Prophet and Islam, and their willingness to sacrifice their lives in the path of defending the religion of God and earning His Paradise.

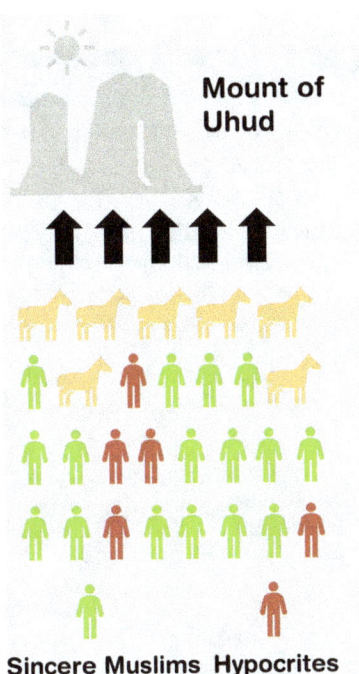

Mount of Uhud

Sincere Muslims Hypocrites

- An army of 1,000 soldiers marched towards Mount Uhud. Some Jewish allies of Abdullah bin Ubayy wanted to join, but the Prophet did not allow them (as per the covenant, they needed the Prophet's permission to enter a battle).
- Making this and the decision to fight outside of the city as an excuse, Abdullah bin Ubayy separated himself along with 300 men and refused to join the Muslims in this battle.
- This act lowered morale among some other soldiers in the army.

- The Prophet gave a speech and explained:
    - Believers do not rely on their numbers and resources, but on Allah when asked by Allah.
    - It is possible that Allah would replace these 300 men with 3,000 angels if Muslims remain steadfast.
- The Prophet began organizing the army and looking over each and every fighter, putting them in an appropriate position. The Prophet positioned his army with Mount Uhud behind him on the right.
- He even refused to put some companions in the battlefield because they were young. He did not allow anyone younger than 15 to fight although many Muslims younger than 15 wanted to participate.
- He installed 50 archers on a small nearby hill, called Jabal Aynayn.
- It is authentically reported via many narrators that the Prophet instructed the leader of the archers, Abdullah bin Jubair, not to leave the position until the battle was over. He said, ""Even if you see the birds eating our bodies, do not leave your places until I send for you."

The Battlefield

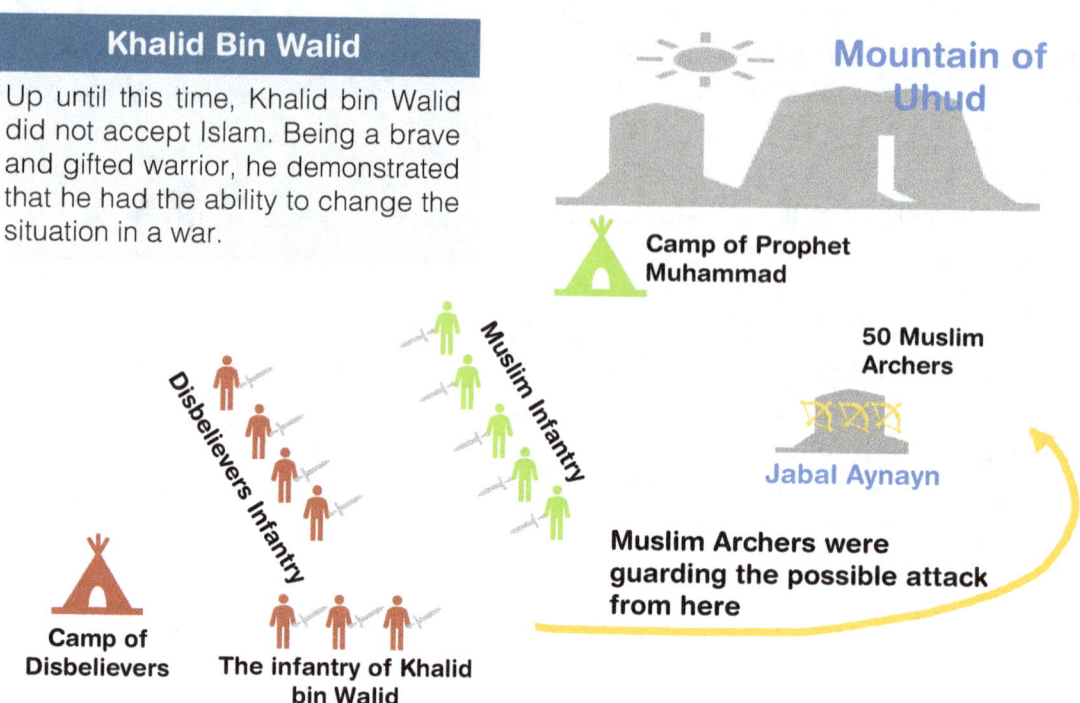

Khalid Bin Walid

Up until this time, Khalid bin Walid did not accept Islam. Being a brave and gifted warrior, he demonstrated that he had the ability to change the situation in a war.

Mountain of Uhud

Camp of Prophet Muhammad

50 Muslim Archers

Jabal Aynayn

Muslim Archers were guarding the possible attack from here

Muslim Infantry

Disbelievers Infantry

Camp of Disbelievers

The infantry of Khalid bin Walid

Four stages of the Battle

1 First Stage

- The Muslims fought fiercely and bravely.
- No flag bearer of the Quraysh could put up resistance against the Muslims – eight of them were killed.
- Companions like Abu Dajanah and Hamza showed great courage and destroyed the enemy's lines.
- The black slave of Jubair bin Mutam, who was guaranteed freedom if he would kill Hamza (because Hamza killed Mutam's uncle in the Battle of Badr), attacked Hamza with his spear, martyred Hamza in the path of God.
- Many Quraysh fighters retreated and ran from the battlefield, which made Muslims think that they had won the battle.
- Many archers left their positions and joined the Muslim army, and started collecting the spoils of war – which was a premature act at that stage.

2 Second Stage

- The battalion of Khalid bin Walid was waiting for this golden moment – they attacked and killed a few remaining archers while Muslims were busy collecting the spoils of war.
- Khalid bin Walid and his men attacked the Muslims from behind and surrounded them. The Muslims panicked due to this calamity.
- For example, a companion named Yaman was killed by the Muslims, even though his son tried to tell them that this was his father.
- To safeguard the Prophet, the companions encircled him, creating a barrier between him and the Quraysh.
- One companion, Ziyad bin Sakan Ansari, took five of his friends, and they attacked the Quraysh to push them away from the Prophet, and all of them died.
- Musab bin Umair also died while protecting the Prophet.
- The Prophet received a wound on his forehead, and his front tooth also broke – some people spread the rumor of the death of the Prophet, which caused more panic among the Muslims.
- Some Muslims wanted to give up after hearing this, but other Muslims encouraged them to continue to fight.

3 Third Stage

- An Ansari, Kaab bin Malik, recognized the Prophet in his war attire and announced that the Prophet was still alive, and everyone should gather around him.
- Quraysh started throwing spears toward the Prophet, which companions like Abu Talha and Abu Dajanah took on their backs.
- The Prophet's face had been pierced by the links of his helmet, which Ubaydah bin Al-Jarrah removed with his teeth, and two of his teeth came out as a result of that.
- Muslims were able to move up the hill with the Prophet and started pelting stones at the Quraysh.
- Abu Sufyan from Quraysh inquired from afar, shouting, whether Muhammad, Abu Bakr, and Omar were still alive. Omar responded, calling him a liar.
- Abu Sufyan tried to give the impression that today they had settled the score of Badr, but Omar told him: "Not even close, our dead are in Heaven and yours in the Hellfire."

- After the Quraysh left the battlefield, the Prophet descended from the hill, identified all the Muslim martyrs, and decided on their collective burial on the battlefield.

- The number of Muslims who died in this battle was between 44 and 70.

- Addressing the Muslims, the Prophet said: "After today, the disbelievers will not be able to gain victory over us again until we kiss the black stone (meaning conquering Makkah).

- Muslims slept peacefully after a long, tiring day in the valley of Uhud.

- The next morning, a rumor spread that Quraysh had decided to come back and attack. The hypocrites played a role in spreading this rumor.

- The Muslims responded that they were ready to fight with the idolaters again if they came back.

- The Prophet set up a small camp and sent out a few people to check the status of Quraysh. Muslims returned to Medina after ensuring that Quraysh had left for Makkah.

وَ لَقَدْ صَدَقَكُمُ اللّٰهُ وَعْدَهُ إِذْ تَحُسُّوْنَهُمْ بِإِذْنِهٖ ۚ حَتّٰى إِذَا فَشِلْتُمْ وَ تَنَازَعْتُمْ فِى الْاَمْرِ وَ عَصَيْتُمْ مِّنْ بَعْدِ مَآ

اَرٰىكُمْ مَّا تُحِبُّوْنَ ۚ مِنْكُمْ مَّنْ يُّرِيْدُ الدُّنْيَا وَ مِنْكُمْ مَّنْ يُّرِيْدُ الْاٰخِرَةَ ۚ ثُمَّ صَرَفَكُمْ عَنْهُمْ لِيَبْتَلِيَكُمْ ۚ وَ لَقَدْ عَفَا

عَنْكُمْ ۗ وَ اللّٰهُ ذُوْ فَضْلٍ عَلَى الْمُؤْمِنِيْنَ إِذْ تُصْعِدُوْنَ وَ لَا تَلْوٗنَ عَلٰى اَحَدٍ وَّ الرَّسُوْلُ يَدْعُوْكُمْ فِىٓ اُخْرٰىكُمْ

فَاَثَابَكُمْ غَمًّا بِغَمٍّ لِّكَيْلَا تَحْزَنُوْا عَلٰى مَا فَاتَكُمْ وَ لَا مَآ اَصَابَكُمْ ۗ وَ اللّٰهُ خَبِيْرٌ بِمَا تَعْمَلُوْنَ

"God did indeed fulfill His promise to you when you, with His permission, were about to destroy your enemy until you flinched and fell to disputing about the matter (archers' position) and disobeyed it after He brought you in sight [of the booty] which you all love. Some of you desire this world, and others desire the Hereafter. Then did He divert you from your foes to test you, but He forgave you: For God is full of grace to those who believe. Remember! You were climbing up the high ground without paying attention to anyone, and the Messenger behind you was calling you back. God gives you one distress after another through payback, to teach you not to distress for [the booty] that had escaped you and for [the ill] that had befallen you. For God is well aware of all that you do." (Surah Aal-e-Imran:152-153)

Analysis of the battle and lessons

The Propaganda of the Enemies

- Through the Battle of Uhud, God wanted to teach the Muslims a lesson, as explained very clearly in the Quran, but the enemies of Islam in Medina painted a completely different picture to create doubts in the people's minds.

Propaganda

- As per them, the Muslims took the beating in this war because:
  - "The Prophet does not listen to anyone, and because of his strategy to fight outside of Medina, he risked the lives of everyone."
  - "God, who helped them in the Battle of Badr, did not come to help."
  - "It was the good strategy, not God's help, which gave Muslims victory in Badr."
  - "The future of Islam after this war is very uncertain."
  - "The promises made in the Quran are just to keep the faithful happy."

Quran's response

- God answered every objection in the Quran.
- The Prophet is the most compassionate person among the Muslims, and he listens to people's advice, but once he decides on something, he does not back off.
- God's help depends on the behavior of the believers.
  - God helped the Muslims in the beginning when Muslims were fighting with full sincerity for the sake of God, without any love for this world in their hearts, obeying the orders of the Prophet, focusing on crushing the enemies of God.
  - But when they disobeyed God's Prophet, left their positions, rushed prematurely to collect the war booty, and panicked, God's help was taken away.
- Regarding the death of many Muslims, God told them that death is imminent, no matter where they are.
- God's promise is still valid, and Muslims will be victorious one day.

Quran's Commentary on Muslims' behavior

- God allowed the defeat because he wanted to separate the people who were not sincere in their religion and fighting to gain worldly benefits (especially hypocrites).
- Piety, discipline, and patience are required throughout the war, not just in a particular portion of the war.
- When the Prophet gives an order, it must not be disobeyed.
- The rush to collect the war booty is an individual act that jeopardizes the collective strategy.
- The war spoils in these wars under the leadership of a Messenger is a favor from God, not because of people's efforts, because if they win with the help of God, they have no full right to the spoils.
- The believers' target should be the Hereafter and the pleasure of God.
- Wins and losses should not be the main reasons to judge the Truth and God's religion.
- If believers make mistakes, they should ask for forgiveness from God rather than lose hope in God's Mercy.
- The Messenger of God will not live forever, so if he dies today, will they turn their back on Islam and God? Their loyalty to God should not be limited to only when the Prophet is living among them.

Significance of the Battle of Uhud

- These are the reasons the Battle of Uhud to be significant for Muslims and the mission of Prophet Muhammad.

Believers and hypocrites are separated	Blessing and help are tied to sincerity toward Allah	Believers must be aware of the role of hypocrites
Difficult times expose strengths & weaknesses	Pay attention to enemies within	Who is ready to sacrifice their lives for the Prophet
Believers may lose seemingly but Allah will always make them victorious	Many more severe tests were on the way for believers, and they must remain sincere to Allah	

Some Notable Incidents

Wahshi, the slave of Jubayr ibn Mutim, the son of Mutim ibn Adi, killed the Prophet's uncle Hamza Bin Abdul Muttalib. In Uhud, Jubayr's uncle, Tuaymah ibn Adi, was killed by Hamzah. So Jubayr wants revenge; he tells his slave Wahshi, "If you kill Hamzah, you will be free." So it's a double revenge: (i) Hamzah killed his uncle, so he wants Hamzah killed, and (ii) just like he lost his uncle, he wants the Prophet to lose his uncle.

A disbeliever, Ubayy bin Khalaf Jumahi, promised Prophet Muhammad during the Battle of Bader that he would kill the Prophet one day, and he is training a horse for this purpose. The Prophet predicted at that time: "No, instead, I will kill you." During the Battle of Uhud, when Ubayy tried to approach the Prophet on the same horse, the companions tried to stop him, but the Prophet asked them to let him come. The Prophet killed him by shooting an arrow at him.

A Jew from the tribe of Banu Thalabah told his tribe to fight along with the Prophet, and helping the Prophet is their duty. The Jews declined to say that it was the day of the Sabbath, and Jews don't fight on this day. He explained that the Sabbath does not place any barrier in fighting for the sake of God. He picked up his battle gear and left for Uhud alone, where he was killed while fighting. When the Prophet heard about him, he said that he was among the best of the Jews.

One of the men, Qazman, fought with great courage and killed many Idolaters. When he was mentioned to the Prophet, the Prophet said he was among the people of Hell. When Qazman was wounded, he was brought to a settlement. People praised him, saying he had shown bravery and should receive predictions of Paradise. Qazman said: "By God! I have fought for the glory of my nation. If it had not come to Uhud, I would not have come either." Later, when the pain from his wounds became severe, he committed suicide with his arrow.

Lesson for us

We lose help from God and His blessings when these two factors are involved in anything that we do:

- Disobey God and His Messenger in the matters that they have already settled.
- The intention is to gain some material benefits of this world instead of pleasing God and earning Paradise in the Hereafter.

Ever-watchful (Observer)

- This attribute of Allah signifies His constant, detailed, and protective observation of all creation.
- His watchfulness is about many aspects:
  - Out of care, similar to a guardian watching over a charge.
  - Not only watchful over deeds but also "thoughts and intentions".
  - Watchful to manage all affairs with "perfect planning and wisdom."
- Allah used this attribute in the Quran when He wants us to be careful and cautious of our actions specially related to Him and our fellow human beings.

يَـٰٓأَيُّهَا النَّاسُ اتَّقُوا رَبَّكُمُ الَّذِى خَلَقَكُم مِّن نَّفْسٍ وَّاحِدَةٍ وَّ خَلَقَ مِنْهَا زَوْجَهَا وَ بَثَّ مِنْهُمَا رِجَالًا كَثِيرًا وَّ نِسَآءً ۚ وَ اتَّقُوا اللّٰهَ الَّذِى تَسَآءَلُوْنَ بِهٖ وَ الْأَرْحَامَ ۚ اِنَّ اللّٰهَ كَانَ عَلَيْكُمْ رَقِيْبًا

O People! Have fear of your Lord Who created you from a single soul and from its genre created its spouse and through these two scattered many men and women [in the earth]. Fear the God whose name you invoke to seek help from one another, and fear breaking relationships. Indeed, God is watching over you. (4:1)

If we must prepare properly to succeed in something, why do we need Allah's help? What is the real concept of *Tawakkul*?

MAP OF THE BATTLE OF UHUD

Hand draw the map of the Battle of Uhud on a paper and write <u>five</u> keywords that define the battle and the lessons we learned from it.

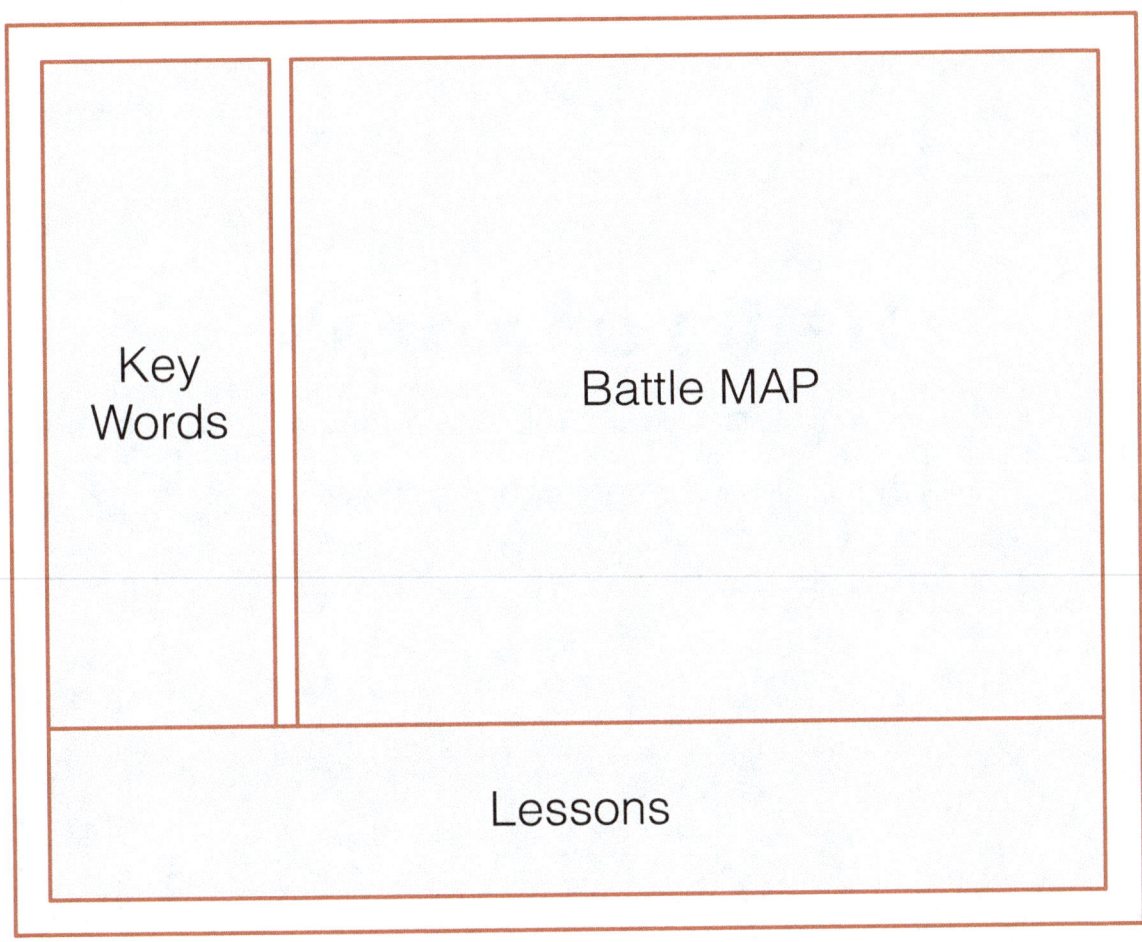

Key Words

Battle MAP

Lessons

Chapter 10

Battle of Ahzab

In this chapter, we will learn about the Battle of Ahzab, also known as the Battle of the Trench. It was considered one of the most difficult tests that believers went through in this mission.

What led to the Battle of Ahzab

The incident near the Well of Maonah

- Before the Battle of Ahzab, an unfortunate incident occurred due to a deceitful scheme plotted by the tribe of Banu Amir with the help of the Jewish tribe Banu Nadheer.
- Abu Baraa bin Malik came to Prophet Muhammad, who invited him to Islam. However, instead, he requested that a group of men be sent to teach Islam to his tribe and the tribes near his own.
- Initially, the Prophet was uncomfortable sending the men, but then Abu Baraa reassured the Prophet of their safety.
- The Prophet sent a group of 40 men to teach Islam to the Banu Amir tribes.
- Banu Amir convinced other tribes to attack the Muslims when they arrived and killed all of them.
- When the Prophet was informed, he made a special dua against all those involved for one month, asking God to punish them.
- Later, it was revealed that the Jewish tribe Banu Nadheer was also behind this scheme.
- The results of the Battle of Uhud encouraged the Jewish tribes, especially the Banu Nadheer, against the Muslims

The Expulsion of Banu Nadheer

- It became apparent that Banu Nadheer was involved in providing logistical support to Quraysh in the Battle of Uhud, and they were also involved in planning the massacre of innocent Muslims.
- When the Prophet went to settle something with Banu Nadheer, they plotted to kill the Prophet by throwing a large rock from above him, but Allah informed him, and he left the area immediately.
- To remove the growing mistrust and to warn the Jews about any negative role against the Muslims, the Prophet decided to renew the covenant that he signed with the Jews of Bani Israel.
- Allah informed the Prophet that the Banu Nadheer are playing the role of Satan, who incites people without coming to the front.
- They even tried to kill the Prophet, and he was left with no choice but to ask Banu Nadheer to leave the area and migrate from the outskirts of Medina to some other place.
- After remaining under siege for more than three weeks and seeing no help from their allies, they accepted the exile on the condition that they would be allowed to take their belongings, which the Prophet accepted.

The enmity of the Jews of Bani Israel

- God talked about their expulsion in Surah Hashr.

$$
\text{هُوَ الَّذِىٓ اَخْرَجَ الَّذِيْنَ كَفَرُوْا مِنْ اَهْلِ الْكِتٰبِ مِنْ دِيَارِهِمْ لِاَوَّلِ الْحَشْرِؕ مَا ظَنَنْتُمْ اَنْ}
$$

$$
\text{يَّخْرُجُوْا وَ ظَنُّوٓا اَنَّهُمْ مَّانِعَتُهُمْ حُصُوْنُهُمْ مِّنَ اللّٰهِ فَاَتٰىهُمُ اللّٰهُ مِنْ حَيْثُ لَمْ يَحْتَسِبُوْا ۪ وَ قَذَفَ}
$$

$$
\text{فِىْ قُلُوْبِهِمُ الرُّعْبَ يُخْرِبُوْنَ بُيُوْتَهُمْ بِاَيْدِيْهِمْ وَ اَيْدِى الْمُؤْمِنِيْنَ ۪ فَاعْتَبِرُوْا يٰٓاُولِى الْاَبْصَارِ}
$$

$$
\text{وَ لَوْ لَآ اَنْ كَتَبَ اللّٰهُ عَلَيْهِمُ الْجَلَآءَ لَعَذَّبَهُمْ فِى الدُّنْيَاؕ وَ لَهُمْ فِى الْاٰخِرَةِ عَذَابُ النَّارِ}
$$

"It is He Who got out the unbelievers among the People of the Book from their homes at the first gathering (of the Muslim army). Little did you think they would escape, and they believed their fortresses would protect them from God. But the (Wrath of) God came to them from places from which they little expected (it), and He cast terror into their hearts, so that they destroyed their dwellings by their own hands and the hands of the believers, take warning, then, people who have understanding! And had it not been that God had decreed exile for them, He would certainly have punished them in this world: And in the Hereafter, they shall (certainly) have the punishment of the fire. That is because they tried to oppose God and His Messenger. And if anyone opposes God, verily God is severe in punishment." **(59:2-4)**

It is reported that the Jews of Bani Israel were expecting a Prophet in this region, as written in their books. However, they anticipated the last Prophet to be among them. Huyayy ibn Akhtab was one of the leaders of Banu Nadheer. His daughter, Safiyyah, who later became the Prophet's wife, narrated a conversation between her father and her uncle, Yasir ibn Akhtab.

She said, "When the Prophet first arrived in Medina, my father and uncle both went to meet him. They both loved me so much and were always playing with me. But when they returned after meeting the Prophet, they entered a room without paying attention to me.

My uncle asked my father, "Is he the one?" My father replied sadly, "By Allah, he is the one." My uncle asked my father, "Then what will you do?" My father said, **"To become his enemy as long as I live,"** meaning he could not accept any non-Jew as the Prophet.

The Battle of Ahzab or Trench

The enemies joined hands

- The following were the enemies of Islam at this stage:
  - Quraysh of Makkah
  - Jews of Bani Israel, especially Banu Nadheer
  - Allies of Quraysh
  - Jews outside of Medinah
- They agreed to bring the entire Arabian Peninsula outside Medina and attack it to finish this threat.
- The Prophet was fully aware of this plot, and he sent small groups of men toward the tribes who agreed to participate with the Jews and warned them of the consequences and a fate similar to that of Quraysh in the Battle of Badr.

How to defend Medinah?

- The Muslims realized that their resources to face the collective strength of the entire Arabia were insufficient, and fighting them would be tough.
- Salman Al-Farsi suggested digging a trench around Medina, covering the sides that are not protected by the mountains or by one of the Muslim allies (the North and West sides of Medina).

- The other sides were either protected by the hard, rocky terrain (lava fields), gardens full of date palms, or the houses of the tribes with which Muslims had signed the agreement.
- The Prophet divided the trench into sections, and a group was assigned to dig that section.
- The Prophet participated in this entire effort and gave them glad tidings that the time was approaching when Muslims would rule Yemen, Persia, and Rome.
- Finally, the enemies arrived on the other side of the trench, surprised.
- The Prophet took an oath from everyone that they would not turn their backs at this critical juncture.
- The Prophet placed a group of 200 men near the dwellings of Banu Qurayzah to keep an eye on them.
- He set up his camp at a place where he could see the entire Medina, which turned into a battlefield.

The Map of the Trench

- The trench was built between the two rocky terrains, which were hard to cross or to position on.
- The map of the battlefield (Medina converted into a battlefield) looks as shown below:

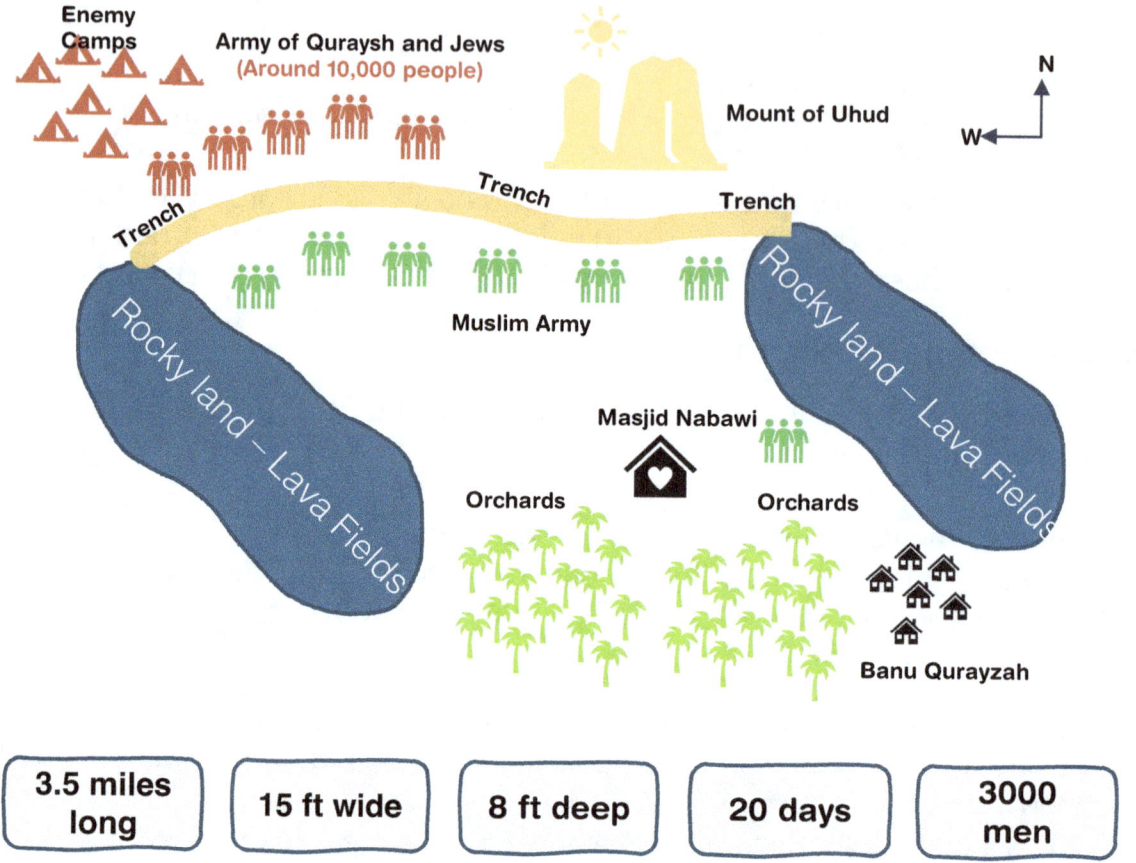

| 3.5 miles long | 15 ft wide | 8 ft deep | 20 days | 3000 men |

Note: Some narrations reported slightly different numbers

Some critics called this a cowardly strategy of people afraid of fighting despite Allah with them. What do you think?

The Siege of Medina

- The Medina was practically cut off from the outside world and was under siege.
- Arab fighters were experts in surrounding the enemy from all sides for physical attack and fighting face to face, but they had never dreamt of the situation they found themselves in here.
- The trench proved to be a barrier because of its depth and breadth. Some brave people tried to cross on horseback, but all of them fell into the ditch.
- Whenever a group of disbelievers tried to come near the trench, the Muslims would target them with their arrows, and they were pushed back.
- Practically, no active fighting was going on, and both armies were camped across the trench in the vast lands of Medina. Both parties were throwing arrows toward each other, which killed a few people on both sides, but there was no chance of a major strike.
- God painted this horrible picture in the Quran.

إِذْ جَآءُوكُمْ مِّنْ فَوْقِكُمْ وَ مِنْ اَسْفَلَ مِنْكُمْ وَ اِذْ زَاغَتِ الْاَبْصَارُ وَ بَلَغَتِ الْقُلُوبُ
الْحَنَاجِرَ وَ تَظُنُّونَ بِاللّٰهِ الظُّنُوْنَا

"Remember, When they came upon you from above you and from below you, and when the eyes became wild (due to fear), and the hearts rose up to the throats, and you imagined various (vain) thoughts about God (Ahzab:10)

Banu Qurayzah violated the Covenant

- The Muslims relied on Banu Qurayzah to prevent any enemy from their side (please see the map), and they remained neutral at first.
- One of the Jewish leaders in Medina, Haye bin Akhtab, planned to divide the Muslims and convinced Banu Qurayzah to violate the agreement. He told them that Quraysh and the Jewish tribes had worked very hard in bringing the entire force of Arabs to the doorsteps of Medina, and Banu Qurayzah must not miss this opportunity to eliminate Islam.
- When the Prophet learned of this discussion, he sent a few Ansar leaders to Banu Qurayzah. Their leader, Kaab bin Asad, showed resistance and even rejected the idea of any agreement signed with Muslims.
- The Ansars returned to the Prophet and informed him privately about the situation. The Prophet made a speech on that occasion and congratulated the Muslims that now God had allowed them to expel the last Jewish tribe from the lands of Medina
- He appointed a platoon of 300 companions to protect Medina from the Banu Qurayzah's side.

The role of the Hypocrites

- The hypocrites within Medina started to spread the message that the promises made by God and His Messenger were a mere illusion.
- Some people said that Muslims were talking about taking over Rome and Persia, but here they are, besieged in this land with no way out.
- The tribes living in the suburbs started to say that 'the people of Yathrib' would never be able to deal with this Arab army.
- The hypocrites who were part of the army started to leave the battlefield to go back to their homes. They tried to persuade Muslims to move to the less active section of the trench.
- Some hypocrites attempted to attack the houses with women and children alone, but the Muslim women and some people from the Muslim army failed those attempts.

Few Miracles of Prophet Muhammad

The wife of one of the companions gave her daughter a few dates in a piece of cloth to give to her father and uncle on the battlefield. The child was looking for them when she passed the Prophet, who asked her what she had in her bundle. She told him they were dates her mother had given her father and uncle. The Prophet took the bundle, asked for a sheet of cloth, and spread the dates. Then he asked a man to call everyone to come and eat them. The army would come, eat, fill themselves, and leave until everyone was satisfied, but the sheet was still overflowing with the dates.

Jabir bin Abdullah whispered to the Prophet that his wife had prepared some food (they had slaughtered a small goat and some bread) and asked him to invite a couple of more people to come and eat. The Prophet stood up and announced, 'O, people of the trench, Jabir and his wife have prepared some food for us, so come and join.' The Prophet told Jabir and his wife not to lift the pot until he came. Then Jabir ran to his house and told his wife that the Prophet had invited everyone. The wife asked, "Did you announce or the Prophet?" he said, "The Prophet." Then his wife said, "Don't worry; there will not be an issue." The Prophet made dua while the pot was still on the stove. Then, 10/20 people came at a time, ate, and left. Jabir mentioned that around 1,000 people ate from that pot that day.

In these circumstances, what role do miracles play for people around the Prophet?

God's help has arrived!

يَآأَيُّهَا الَّذِينَ ءَامَنُوا اذْكُرُوا نِعْمَةَ اللّهِ عَلَيْكُمْ إِذْ جَآءَتْكُمْ جُنُودٌ فَأَرْسَلْنَا عَلَيْهِمْ رِيحًا وَّ جُنُودًا لَّمْ تَرَوْهَا ۚ وَ كَانَ اللّهُ بِمَا تَعْمَلُونَ بَصِيرًا

Believers, recall God's favor upon you when the army attacked you. We sent a wind and the armies, which you could not see, to support you. God sees all that you do. (Ahzab:9)

- It was winter, and the disbelievers were growing irritated and tired from a siege that had lasted more than 3 weeks. Many believers sacrificed their lives, and some got injured due to flying arrows coming from the other side.
- The Prophet was making this dua: "O Allah! He who has revealed the Quran and who will settle scores quickly, please defeat the enemy's combined forces. O Allah, defeat them and cause them to stumble and disintegrate."
- Finally, the unseen armies of God came into action, and a cold, stormy wind blew over them constantly, making it harder for the disbelievers to remain out in the open for long. It uprooted their tents and covering, leaving them with no shelter.
- The enemies started to flee in flocks toward their homes. When the night was over, Muslims could not believe the army had already left.
- God helped Prophet Muhammad and Muslims and destroyed the enemies' grand scheme and their efforts.

Dealing with Banu Qurayzah

- Immediately after the Battle of Ahzab concluded, the Prophet surrounded the settlement of Banu Qurayzah and laid siege to it for more than 25 days.
- Their leader, Kaab bin Asad, suggested they could accept Islam or the punishment of treason as per Jewish law. The Jews were, however, not ready to take any of these ideas. The Jewish leaders accepted that whatever decision the leader of Aws, Saad bin Muad (Ansari, who was injured in the battle of Ahzab), made would be accepted by Banu Qurayzah.
- Saad bin Muad, who was receiving treatment in Masjid e Nabawi, was brought to the site. Saad asked Banu Qurayzah if his decision would be accepted, and they said yes. Saad decided, as per the laws of the Jews, which suggested that all men of the tribe were to be killed, women and children would be captured, and their property confiscated.
- This punishment for treason was implemented as described in the Torah.

Lessons learned

Good news from Prophet Muhammad

- After the Battle of the Trench (or Ahzab), the Prophet gave the good news to the Muslims: "Now we shall fight with them. They will not fight with us."
- He also said God purified Medina by removing Jews who were wolves in sheep's clothing.
- The attacks of the Quraysh ended with the Battle of Ahzab. The Prophet predicted that the strength of the Quraysh had lessened.
- After the Battles of Badr, Uhud, and Ahzab, the Jewish opposition also came to an end, and they were subsequently exiled.

Lessons for us

- Islam does not sensationalize the news of evil even if it is true. We are not supposed to go telling everybody bad news, even if it is true.
- Here, the Banu Qurayza have cheated, but the Prophet told the leaders of the Ansar to keep it low and asked them not tell everybody.
- This is in complete contrast to all the news spread through various types of social media we see today, where every shocking, juicy matter, rumor, and scandal is analyzed, exposed, and spread to gain political or other benefits. This is harmful for society.
- The decision to dig a trench, a previously unfamiliar defensive tactic to the Arabs, shows the importance of creative thinking and adaptability.
- Not every battle must be fought to spill blood. Sometimes, avoiding a fight is the best strategy for winning.
- Prophet Muhammad's active participation in manual labor, such as carrying soil, exemplifies leadership that manages through direct involvement rather than issuing orders alone.
- Muslims faced intense hunger, cold, and a month-long siege; historians point to their endurance as an excellent example for maintaining faith in the "darkest moments."
- The battle serves as a primary example of balancing practical preparation with ultimate trust in God's support. Success is viewed as a result of both extreme human effort and divine intervention.

The Disposer of Affairs

- God did not just create this Universe, but He also manages it and conducts all its affairs.
- We must have unshakeable trust in Him when something happens to us, and we ask for His help.
- We are asked to do our best and then rely on God; when the result comes, we should accept it, believing it was the best for us.
- Believers, when faced with difficult situations, trust Allah for His help after making all their efforts, by saying **"Hasbunallah u Wa Naimal Wakeel".**

"Allah is sufficient for us, and He is the best Disposer of affairs."

A man stopped at Masjid An-Nabawi and saw the Prophet. He wanted to go inside the mosque and pray, so he asked the Prophet, "Should I tie my camel or trust in God that it will not go anywhere?" The Prophet responded, "Tie the camel and then trust in God." (Sunan Al Tirmidhi #2517)

This hadith shows the best definition of trust in Allah. We should only trust in Allah after doing our part.

SEERAH ACTIVITY

BATTLE OF TRENCH – TEAM DEBATE

Imagine living in Medina at that time. You have been asked to provide a strategy. Some people are in favor of digging the trench, and some are against it. Create two teams and discuss the plan (for and against). Keep the following in mind when debating it:

1. Muslims must plan a course of action through mutual consultation.
2. Every objective can be achieved through multiple courses of action.
3. Winning does not always require fighting.
4. The enemy army was 10,000 strong, and the Muslims were poor with few resources.
5. They had to protect themselves and their families.
6. The enemy was planning to attack from multiple sides.
7. Not all Muslims living in Medina were very devout.
8. Muslims trust in Allah SWT, especially when the Prophet was among them.
9. Muslims have won battles before with a few resources.
10. Planning to defend a city is typically a challenging task.
11. One mistake that would allow the enemy into the city could prove to be fatal for the Muslims.

Chapter 11

Defaming the family of Prophet Muhammad

In this chapter, we will learn about the tactics that Jews and their supporters used as the last resort to counter Islam and Muslims after being defeated on every front.

Enemies Next Strategy

- The enemies of Islam confronted Prophet Muhammad and his companions with an army and a large force of tribes, but failed to defeat them.
- They realized that Prophet Muhammad and the believers are known for their noble character, so now they should attack their honor and destroy their reputations for morality and piety.
- That is the lowest any human being can go in enmity.

The Jews and the Hypocrites tried many techniques to destroy the moral reputation of the Prophet and the believers. This strategy reflects a sick mindset, desperate to see some 'victory' to satisfy its ego.

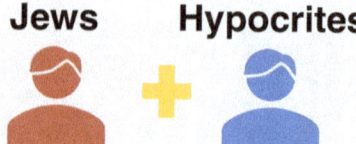

1. Allegations against Muslim Women

- The hypocrites spread scandalous gossip about Muslim men and women.
- Muslim women usually adopt certain etiquette in front of men who are not part of their families. The hypocrites would deliberately try to speak in the presence of the female members of the Prophet's household.
- They used to joke and pass unseemly remarks about women going outside, but when they were admonished for this behavior, they would give the excuse that they were slave women or one of their relatives.
- This situation of harassment continued for some time until the Quran gave some special instructions to the Muslims to handle this situation.

Instructions by the Quran to counter the tactic

- Discourage visits from strangers (not relatives) to their homes.
- Muslim women should not come in front of non-relatives, especially if they have beautified themselves; similarly, men would not interact with non-relative women without any reason.
- If the Prophet has invited people to his house for a reason, they should limit their interaction to the issue at hand and avoid staying there unnecessarily.

- If the Prophet is not at home and someone needs to ask the Prophet's wives something, they will do so from behind a curtain.
- Muslim women were asked to wear a shawl to cover their heads and upper bodies to distinguish themselves from slave women.
- Hypocrites were warned of a painful punishment if they did not change their behavior in this regard, and the Prophet was asked to take action against them at the societal /state level.
- If anyone blames a man or a woman for immoral behavior, the accuser will be asked to bring four witnesses as proof or be ready to face 80 lashes if they fail to do so.

> "Extraordinary times call for extraordinary measures."

يَاأَيُّهَا النَّبِيُّ قُلْ لِّأَزْوَاجِكَ وَ بَنَاتِكَ وَ نِسَاءِ الْمُؤْمِنِينَ يُدْنِينَ عَلَيْهِنَّ مِنْ جَلَابِيبِهِنَّ ذَلِكَ أَدْنَى أَنْ يُعْرَفْنَ فَلَا يُؤْذَيْنَ وَ كَانَ اللَّهُ غَفُورًا رَّحِيمًا لَئِنْ لَّمْ يَنْتَهِ الْمُنَافِقُونَ وَ الَّذِينَ فِى قُلُوبِهِمْ مَّرَضٌ وَّ الْمُرْجِفُونَ فِى الْمَدِينَةِ لَنُغْرِيَنَّكَ بِهِمْ ثُمَّ لَا يُجَاوِرُونَكَ فِيهَا إِلَّا قَلِيلًا مَّلْعُونِينَ أَيْنَمَا ثُقِفُوا أُخِذُوا وَ قُتِّلُوا تَقْتِيلً

"O Prophet! Tell your wives and daughters, and the believing women, that they should put on their outer garments [like a shawl when going outdoors]: that is most appropriate, that they should be known [as believing women] and not harassed. And God is Oft-Forgiving, Most Merciful. Truly, if the Hypocrites, and those in whose hearts is a disease, and those who stir up troublemaking in the City, do not stop, We shall certainly raise you (O Prophet) against them: Then will they not be able to stay in this city as your neighbors for any length of time: They shall have a curse on them: whenever they are found, they shall be seized and punished (with capital punishment) without mercy." **(Ahzab:59-61)**

2. Creating discord between husband and wife

- The Prophet and his wives always led a simple lifestyle.
- The hypocritical women suggested to the wives of the Prophet that they belong to elite families and their honor and dignity demand that they should lead a comfortable life.

Remember: Loving families are the backbone of a prosperous and healthy society.

- They suggested that the wives could at least demand that the Prophet show some generosity in their monthly expenses.
- When some of the wives of the Prophet were influenced by this constant 'preaching,' they talked to the Prophet about increasing their allowances.
- The Prophet's feelings got hurt by listening to such a demand, and he isolated himself for a few days in a separate quarter from all the wives.
- The Prophet remained in isolation for almost a month until the Quran provided him with a solution, and he presented that solution in front of his wives.
- The Quran also advised the wives of the Prophet to avoid meeting the hypocrites, who have a disease of hatred in their hearts.

A fair suggestion given by the Quran

- The Quran made a fair suggestion that the Prophet would give all of his wives these options:

    1 - The Prophet will provide them with some money and divorce them.

    2 - They would remain with the Prophet through thick and thin.

يَآأَيُّهَا النَّبِيُّ قُل لِّأَزْوَاجِكَ اِن كُنْتُنَّ تُرِدْنَ الْحَيَوةَ الدُّنْيَا وَ زِينَتَهَا فَتَعَالَيْنَ أُمَتِّعْكُنَّ وَ أُسَرِّحْكُنَّ سَرَاحًا جَمِيْلً

وَ اِن كُنْتُنَّ تُرِدْنَ اللَّهَ وَ رَسُوْلَهُ وَ الدَّارَ الْأَخِرَةَ فَإِنَّ اللَّهَ اَعَدَّ لِلْمُحْسِنَاتِ مِنْكُنَّ اَجْرًا عَظِيْمًا

"O Prophet! Say to your wives: "If you desire the life of this World and its glitter,- then alright! I will give you some riches and set you free handsomely. But if you seek God and His Messenger, and the home of the Hereafter, indeed God has prepared a great reward for the well-doers amongst you." (Ahzab:28-29)

- Omar's daughter, Hafsa, was also one of the wives of the Prophet, and Omar was very upset with the situation – he thought that the Prophet had divorced all his wives, but the Prophet clarified that he did not.
- However, when presented with options, all of them said they prefer the companionship of the Prophet in this world and the Hereafter over any riches of this world.
- This way, the Quran emphasized to the Prophet's wives that they are not ordinary women and that they should be grateful to God for being the Prophet's wives.
- They were also told that this was a temporary life and God had prepared the best places in Paradise as a reward for being the righteous wives of the Prophet.

O Wives of the Prophet! You are not like any other woman.... (33:32)

يٰنِسَآءَ النَّبِيِّ لَسْتُنَّ كَأَحَدٍ مِّنَ النِّسَآءِ

3. Marrying the divorcee of the adopted son

- The custom of the society at that time was that the adopted sons were taken as the blood son, so marrying their divorced wives was not allowed.
- The situation is depicted in the pictures below through an example:

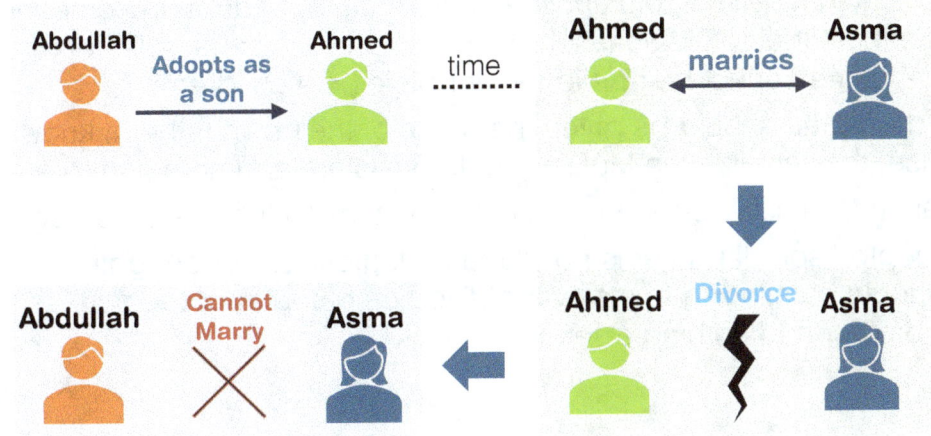

- When the Prophet married Khadijah, she had a slave, Zaid bin Haritha, who continued to live with them after the marriage, and the Prophet adopted him as his son after freeing him later.
- After the Prophethood, he influenced his paternal cousin, Zaynab bint Jahash, to marry Zaid for the following reasons:
- He wanted to elevate Zaid's status from a freed slave to a respectable man who married into the family of Quraysh.
- He wanted to convey to society that, in God's eyes, all humanity is equal.
- Both Zaid and Zaynab accepted the decision of the Prophet out of their love and respect for the Prophet, but both knew that it would require a change in their mentality to carry on as husband and wife.
- They tried to make this relationship work for almost a year, but it did not work out, and despite all the Prophet's efforts, Zaid divorced Zaynab.
- To the Prophet's surprise, Allah asked the Prophet Muhammad to marry Zaynab, which was not acceptable in society at that time.

The hypocrites started to spread the propaganda that the Prophet married his daughter-in-law, and it was a 'shameless' act.

Quran's instructions about child adoption

- The Quran told Muslims, and society in general, that adopting someone does not make them their biological son/daughter, and the same rules of marriage and inheritance cannot be applied as for biological children.
- Adopted children should be given the name of their own father if known. Otherwise, they are like the Muslim brothers/sisters and nothing more.
- This clarifies the situation as shown in the picture on the previous page.
- If the adopted son/daughter is not like a biological son or daughter, then the father should be allowed to marry the divorcee of the adopted son, as he was just his brother and nothing else.

مَا جَعَلَ اللّٰهُ لِرَجُلٍ مِّنْ قَلْبَيْنِ فِیْ جَوْفِهٖ ۚ وَ مَا جَعَلَ اَزْوَاجَكُمُ الّٰٓئِیْ تُظٰهِرُوْنَ مِنْهُنَّ اُمَّهٰتِكُمْ ۚ وَ مَا جَعَلَ اَدْعِیَآءَكُمْ اَبْنَآءَكُمْ ۚ ذٰلِكُمْ قَوْلُكُمْ بِاَفْوَاهِكُمْ ۚ وَ اللّٰهُ یَقُوْلُ الْحَقَّ وَ هُوَ یَهْدِی السَّبِیْلَ اُدْعُوْهُمْ لِاٰبَآئِهِمْ هُوَ اَقْسَطُ عِنْدَ اللّٰهِ ۚ فَاِنْ لَّمْ تَعْلَمُوْۤا اٰبَآءَهُمْ فَاِخْوَانُكُمْ فِی الدِّیْنِ وَ مَوَالِیْكُمْ ۚ وَ لَیْسَ عَلَیْكُمْ جُنَاحٌ فِیْمَاۤ اَخْطَاْتُمْ بِهٖ ۙ وَ لٰكِنْ مَّا تَعَمَّدَتْ قُلُوْبُكُمْ ۚ وَ كَانَ اللّٰهُ غَفُوْرًا رَّحِیْمًا

"God has not made two hearts in his body for any man: nor has He made your wives whom you divorce by *Zihar* your mothers: **nor has He made your adopted sons your sons.** Such is [only] your [manner of] speech coming from your mouths. But God tells [you] the Truth, and He shows the [right) Way. **Call them (adopted sons) by their fathers: that is more just in the sight of God. But if you do not know their father, then they are your brothers in faith or your friends.** But there is no blame on you if you make a mistake therein: [what counts is] the intention of your hearts: and God is Oft-Returning, Most Merciful." (Ahzab:4-5)

4. Targeting Prophet's multiple marriages

- Before marrying Zaynab, the Prophet already had four wives.
- Marrying more than one woman at a time was a common practice in that society, and people married many wives without restriction on the number. Islam restricted that number to four wives at a time.
- When the Prophet married Zaynab, the hypocrites found another point that they could use to spread malicious propaganda against the Prophet.
- They said: "He is not a true Prophet because he made laws for the Muslims but refused to implement them upon himself. He had restricted all the Muslims to four wives, but he himself does not want to restrict himself to four wives."

Quran's Response

- As expected, Prophet Muhammad did not have to say anything on this matter, as God responded to it.
- God said in the Quran that He has granted the Prophet special permission to marry more than one woman and gave him special laws governing his marriages alone.
- This happened because God asked Prophet Muhammad to marry a few women due to his status as a Messenger, not because Prophet Muhammad wanted to.

يَٰٓأَيُّهَا ٱلنَّبِىُّ إِنَّآ أَحْلَلْنَا لَكَ أَزْوَٰجَكَ ٱلَّٰتِىٓ ءَاتَيْتَ أُجُورَهُنَّ وَ مَا مَلَكَتْ يَمِينُكَ مِمَّآ أَفَآءَ ٱللَّهُ عَلَيْكَ وَ بَنَٰتِ عَمِّكَ وَ بَنَٰتِ عَمَّٰتِكَ وَ بَنَٰتِ خَالِكَ وَ بَنَٰتِ خَٰلَٰتِكَ ٱلَّٰتِى هَاجَرْنَ مَعَكَ وَ ٱمْرَأَةً مُّؤْمِنَةً إِن وَهَبَتْ نَفْسَهَا لِلنَّبِىِّ إِنْ أَرَادَ ٱلنَّبِىُّ أَن يَسْتَنكِحَهَا خَالِصَةً لَّكَ مِن دُونِ ٱلْمُؤْمِنِينَ قَدْ عَلِمْنَا مَا فَرَضْنَا عَلَيْهِمْ فِىٓ أَزْوَٰجِهِمْ وَ مَا مَلَكَتْ أَيْمَٰنُهُمْ لِكَيْلَا يَكُونَ عَلَيْكَ حَرَجٌ وَ كَانَ ٱللَّهُ غَفُورًا رَّحِيمًا

"O Prophet! We have made lawful for you your wives to whom you have paid their dowers; and the female prisoners of war whom God has assigned to you; and daughters of your paternal uncles and aunts, and daughters of your maternal uncles and aunts, who migrated [from Makkah] with you; and any believing woman who dedicates herself to the Prophet if the Prophet wishes to wed her. This is ONLY for you, and not for the other believers; We know what we have appointed for them as to their wives and the female prisoners of war, so that there should be no difficulty for you (to perform your duty as the last Prophet). And God is Oft-Forgiving, Most Merciful." (Ahzab:50)

5. Creating disharmony between Ansar and Migrants

- Prophet Muhammad transformed the historical enmity between Aws and Khazraj into a strong bond of brotherhood among them and with the migrants.

- The Jews and hypocrites were looking for opportunities to create discord among these various groups to achieve their wicked goals.

- During a battle with Bani Mustalaq, while Muslims were camping there, a fight broke out between a migrant and an Ansari, and the migrant slapped the Ansari.

- Abdullah bin Ubayy, the chief of the hypocrites, made an all-out effort to incite the violence between them – he addressed the Ansars, "We have sheltered them, and now they have turned against us. It is true that if you feed a dog, it will turn and bite you. When we return to Medina, the honorable among us should evict these wretched people. This is your fault, O Ansar!"

Prophet Muhammad and Quran's Response

- Prophet Muhammad was informed of the situation, and he immediately took steps to prevent the conflict.

- He confronted the groups, condemning their actions and statements as "statements of the Days of Ignorance" (Jahiliyyah).

- He advised them that such disputes should not arise and that all Muslims should treat each other as brothers, emphasizing the unity of the new community.

- The Quran emphasized the same.

إِنَّمَا الْمُؤْمِنُونَ إِخْوَةٌ فَأَصْلِحُوا بَيْنَ أَخَوَيْكُمْ وَاتَّقُوا اللَّهَ لَعَلَّكُمْ تُرْحَمُونَ

The believers are but brothers, so make reconciliation between your brothers and fear Allah that you may receive mercy. **(Al-Hujrat 10)**

6. Slandering the beloved wife of the Prophet

- On the way back from Bani Mustalaq, the caravan encamped overnight outside Medinah, and Aisha, the Prophet's wife who had accompanied him on this journey, walked away from the army to relieve herself (possibly in the morning, though it was still dark).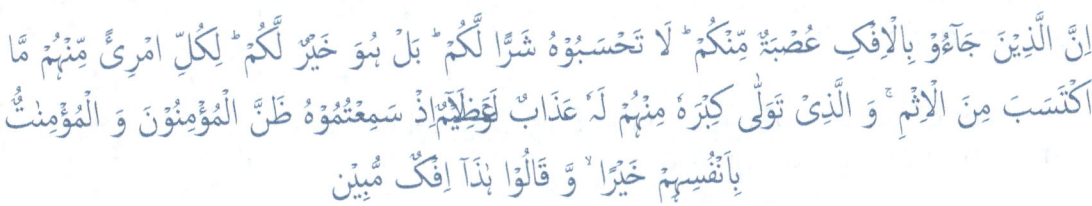

- While she was coming back, she realized that she had lost her onyx necklace, so she went back to look for it.

- When she came back, she noticed that nobody was there, and everyone had left, thinking she was already inside the tent.

- Safwan bin Muattal, who stayed behind the caravan, found her there alone and took her with him back to Medina after learning what had happened to her.

- The chief of the hypocrites, Abdullah bin Ubayy, turned this whole episode into a big scandal.

- Some Muslims were also influenced as a result of the gossip against the family of the Prophet.

- The Prophet remained disturbed for almost a month. And this whole ordeal made Aisha sick in bed.

Quran's Response

- Once again, the Quran came to protect the honor of Aisha, the wife of Prophet Muhammad.

- At the same time, the Quran admonished the Muslims who fell into the trap laid by the hypocrites.

اِنَّ الَّذِيْنَ جَآءُوْ بِالْاِفْكِ عُصْبَةٌ مِّنْكُمْ لَا تَحْسَبُوْهُ شَرًّا لَّكُمْ بَلْ هُوَ خَيْرٌ لَّكُمْ لِكُلِّ امْرِئٍ مِّنْهُمْ مَّا اكْتَسَبَ مِنَ الْاِثْمِ وَ الَّذِىْ تَوَلّٰى كِبْرَهٗ مِنْهُمْ لَهٗ عَذَابٌ عَظِيْمٌ اِذْ سَمِعْتُمُوْهُ ظَنَّ الْمُؤْمِنُوْنَ وَ الْمُؤْمِنٰتُ بِاَنْفُسِهِمْ خَيْرًا وَّ قَالُوْا هٰذَآ اِفْكٌ مُّبِيْنٌ

Undoubtedly, those who have fabricated this slander are among you. Do not think this to be a misfortune for you; it is, in fact, better for you. The sin each of them has earned will be placed in his account, and for [the originator of this mischief] who has the most significant share in it, from among them, there is a great torment. When you people heard this, why did you not believe men and believing women think graciously in favor of their people, and why did they not say: "This is an open slander." (24:11-12)

The evils of society

Gossip and Slandering

- Gossip is a close cousin to slander – both aim to spread news that damages others' honor. However slander is worst than gossiping but gossip causes it. It is usually the pastime of people who do not care about others.
- It harms the honor, reputation, and feelings of others, knowingly or unknowingly, which is a serious sin.
- It is a type of bullying in which the subject has no way to defend himself/herself.
- God has asked Muslims to stay away from: Anything that does not concern them, suspicion, gossip, backbiting.
- When you hear something that might hurt other people's honor: Encourage people not to talk about it, do not spread it to other people, do not try to investigate it if it does not directly concern you.

Guidance from the Quran and Sunnah

يَٰٓأَيُّهَا الَّذِينَ آمَنُوا اجْتَنِبُوا كَثِيرًا مِّنَ الظَّنِّ اِنَّ بَعْضَ الظَّنِّ اِثْمٌ وَّ لَا تَجَسَّسُوا وَ لَا يَغْتَب بَّعْضُكُم بَعْضًا اَيُحِبُّ اَحَدُكُمْ اَنْ يَّأْكُلَ لَحْمَ اَخِيهِ مَيْتًا فَكَرِهْتُمُوهُ وَ اتَّقُوا اللّٰهَ اِنَّ اللّٰهَ تَوَّابٌ رَّحِيمٌ

Believers! Refrain from too much suspicion because some suspicions are pure sins. And do not spy [on others] and do not indulge in backbiting one another. Is there anyone among you who would like to eat the meat of his dead brother? So, you do not tolerate this; [then why should backbiting be tolerated!] Fear God. God surely is quick in accepting repentance, Ever-Merciful. (49:12)

"From the excellence of a man's Islam is leaving that which does not concern him."

"Whoever believes in Allah and the Last Day, let him say something good or remain silent."

- Why is a happy and loving family the most important unit of a healthy society?
- What role does social media play in gossip and slander?

The Marriages of the Prophet

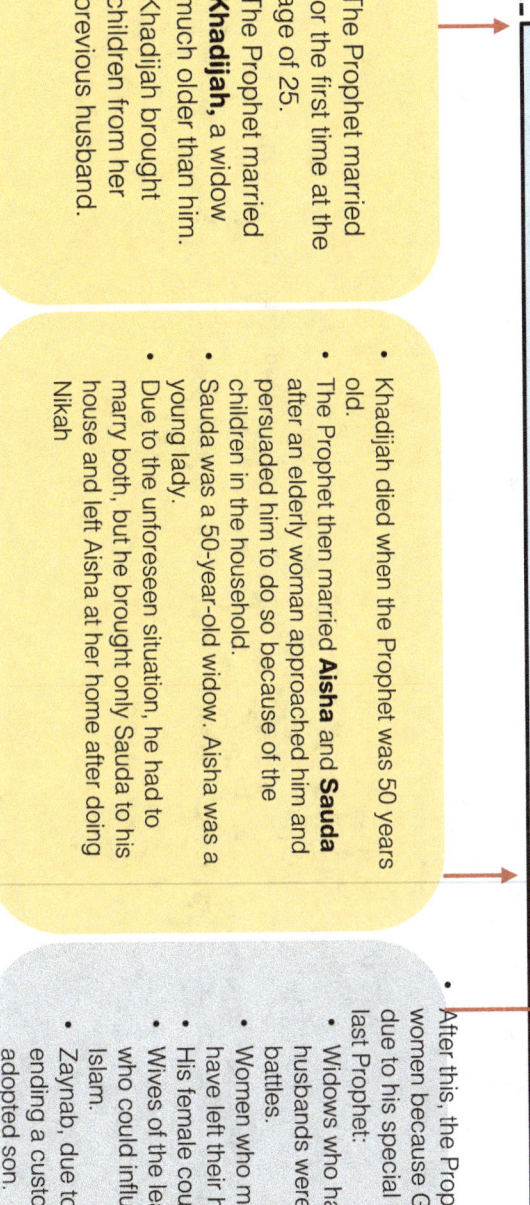

Age 25

- The Prophet married for the first time at the age of 25.
- The Prophet married **Khadijah**, a widow much older than him.
- Khadijah brought children from her previous husband.

Khadijah remained his only wife in this period (25 years) until she died just 1 or 2 years before the Hijrah. In Arab society, it was normal for a man to marry more than one woman. The Prophet did not do so. All his children were from Khadijah.

- Khadijah died when the Prophet was 50 years old.
- The Prophet then married **Aisha** and **Sauda** after an elderly woman approached him and persuaded him to do so because of the children in the household.
- Sauda was a 50-year-old widow. Aisha was a young lady.
- Due to the unforeseen situation, he had to marry both, but he brought only Sauda to his house and left Aisha at her home after doing Nikah

During that time (3 years), he had two wives. Sauda was living with him, and Aisha was living at her house. When Aisha's father, Abu Bakr, asked him to take her to his home, he first asked Sauda if that was OK with her. She agreed, so the Prophet brought Aisha to another house (a separate small quarter). These are all the marriages (Khadijah, Sauda, Aisha) that the Prophet had with his intentions.

Age 50   **Age 54**   **9 years**   **Age 63**

Death

- After this, the Prophet married 8 more women because God told him to do so due to his special responsibilities as the last Prophet:
- Widows who had kids and their husbands were martyred in the battles.
- Women who migrated with him and have left their husbands.
- His female cousins want to marry him.
- Wives of the leaders from other tribes who could influence the spread of Islam.
- Zaynab, due to the special situation of ending a custom related to the adopted son.

Wives of the Prophet

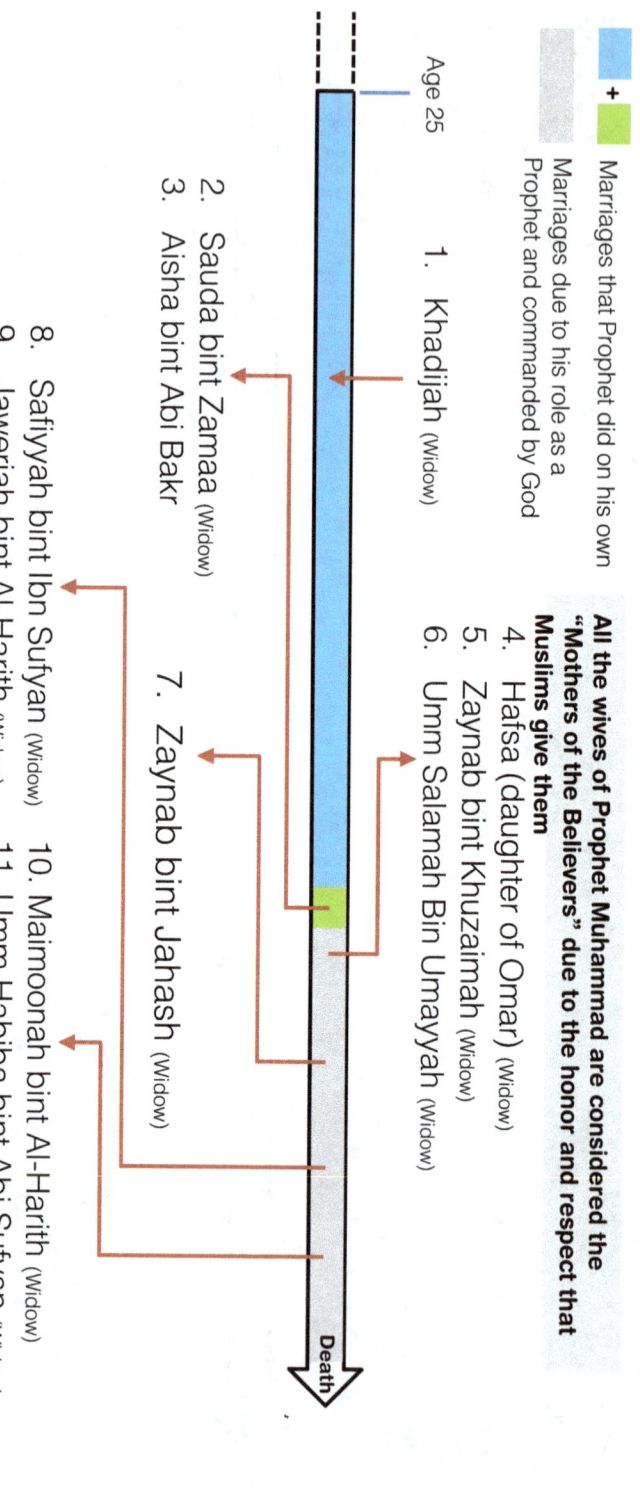

+

Marriages that Prophet did on his own

Marriages due to his role as a
Prophet and commanded by God

Age 25

1. Khadijah (Widow)

2. Sauda bint Zamaa (Widow)
3. Aisha bint Abi Bakr

8. Safiyyah bint Ibn Sufyan (Widow)
9. Jaweriah bint Al-Harith (Widow)

7. Zaynab bint Jahash (Widow)

**All the wives of Prophet Muhammad are considered the
"Mothers of the Believers" due to the honor and respect that
Muslims give them**

4. Hafsa (daughter of Omar) (Widow)
5. Zaynab bint Khuzaimah (Widow)
6. Umm Salamah Bin Umayyah (Widow)

10. Maimoonah bint Al-Harith (Widow)
11. Umm Habiba bint Abi Sufyan (Widow)

Death

Summary

- The Jews and the hypocrites tried to attack the Muslims and the Prophet from the moral side and attempted to destroy their honor and respect in society, but the truth always prevailed, and they failed miserably.
- Through these events, God exposed the enemies of Islam from within.
- The result of the mischief planned by the hypocrites through these events was contrary to what they had planned to achieve, and Muslims came out of this test much stronger than before.
- At the same time, the Muslims learned great moral lessons from these events specially those that make a society corrupt and weak.

The All-Strong

- Allah is All-Strong with no sign of weakness.
- His strength is supreme and unlimited.
- He does not grow weary of running the affairs of this world.
- We can observe some of His powers in the form of strong winds and the sea, which, in its nature, is made of subtle entities like air and water, but they can destroy buildings and lift heavy objects like trucks and ships.
- Sometimes, we feel that, despite being All-Strong, Allah does not intervene, especially in cases of injustice committed against weaker human beings. That is not due to any weakness, but because Allah has made this world a test, which demands that He not interfere in everything.
- If we really want to understand the strength of Allah, we should see his huge universe and how it is created. It created a sense of awe for Allah in us.
- The verse below reminded us that we do not give due respect and value to Allah.

يَٰٓأَيُّهَا النَّاسُ ضُرِبَ مَثَلٌ فَاسْتَمِعُوا لَهُ ۚ إِنَّ الَّذِينَ تَدْعُونَ مِن دُونِ اللَّهِ لَن يَخْلُقُوا ذُبَابًا وَّ لَوِ اجْتَمَعُوا لَهُ ۚ وَ إِن يَسْلُبْهُمُ الذُّبَابُ شَيْئًا لَّا يَسْتَنقِذُوهُ مِنْهُ ۚ ضَعُفَ الطَّالِبُ وَ الْمَطْلُوبُ مَا قَدَرُوا اللَّهَ حَقَّ قَدْرِهِ ۚ إِنَّ اللَّهَ لَقَوِيٌّ عَزِيزٌ

People! An example is cited: So, listen to it attentively. In reality, those whom you invoke besides God cannot create even a fly, even if all of them try to. And if that fly snatches something from them, they cannot even snatch it back. Those who desire are frail, and what they desire is absolutely frail too. They have not recognized the value of God the way it should be. Indeed, God is All-Strong and All-Powerful. (22:73-74)

SEERAH ACTIVITY

GOSSIP OR TRUTH SORTING GAME

Please copy this page or color the card tabs within the book according to the correct bucket you think they belong in.

Hasan said, the school might close early next week	I think the substitute teacher is spying on us	Sara said something bad about Islam yesterday
Fatimah recited Surah Al-Fajr in class today	Aisha always brags about her grades.	There are around 6500 verses in the Quran
Nobody likes sitting with Musa — he smells weird.	The Battle of Uhud happened after the Battle of Badr	Hassan eats like a baby and makes noises at lunch.
I think Mariam only pretends to be nice in front of the teacher	Zaynab talks too much when the teacher isn't looking.	The teacher is strict; she hates boys
Bilal helps set up chairs before school starts	The Prophet was kind even to those who hurt him	I heard someone say that Jamal is getting kicked out of class
Yasmin may have stolen money from the charity box	Hamza was cheating in the test — I know it	Ali doesn't even pray at home

Our class will go on a field trip next Sunday	Someone told me this hadith is not true

 Truth  Gossip  Slander  Verify

Chapter 12

Treaty of Hudaybiyah

In this chapter, we will learn about the Treaty of Hudaybiyah, which the Quran called a clear victory, and changed the entire situation of Islam and Muslims in the Arabian Peninsula

Muslims went for the Umrah

- The entire episode of the Treaty of Hudaybiyah occurred because the Muslims planned an Umrah visit to Makkah under the leadership of the Prophet Muhammad.

The Dream of Prophet Muhammad

- A year after the Battle of Ahzab, the Prophet saw a dream in which he entered the Kabaah with his companions, their heads shaved, as is usually done during Umrah (if performed outside Dhul Hijjah).
- Even though the political situation with Quraysh was not favorable for this Umrah trip, he and his companions considered it a command from God.

A Prophet's dream is a form of revelation from God.

- The believers got overjoyed when they heard that they would be going to Kabaah.
- The hypocrites and weak Muslims started creating doubts and fear, and considered this journey as committing suicide (In Ihram, a person can carry only one sword in its sheath as per the Islamic law). They avoided this journey and stayed at home.

بَلْ ظَنَنْتُمْ اَنْ لَّنْ يَّنْقَلِبَ الرَّسُوْلُ وَ الْمُؤْمِنُوْنَ اِلٰٓى اَهْلِيْهِمْ اَبَدًا وَّ زُيِّنَ ذٰلِكَ فِىْ قُلُوْبِكُمْ وَ ظَنَنْتُمْ ظَنَّ السَّوْءِ ۚ وَ كُنْتُمْ قَوْمًا بُوْرًا

"No, but you all thought that the Messenger and the believers would never return to their families (from this trip); this seemed pleasing in your hearts, and you conceived an evil thought, for you are a people who will be doomed. **(48:12)**

لَقَدْ صَدَقَ اللّٰهُ رَسُوْلَهُ الرُّءْيَا بِالْحَقِّ ۚ لَتَدْخُلُنَّ الْمَسْجِدَ الْحَرَامَ اِنْ شَآءَ اللّٰهُ اٰمِنِيْنَ ۙ مُحَلِّقِيْنَ رُءُوْسَكُمْ وَ مُقَصِّرِيْنَ ۙ لَا تَخَافُوْنَ ۚ فَعَلِمَ مَا لَمْ تَعْلَمُوْا فَجَعَلَ مِنْ دُوْنِ ذٰلِكَ فَتْحًا قَرِيْبًا

[So, rest assured O Believers!] it is a fact that God had shown His messenger an absolutely true dream. Indeed, if God wills, you will definitely enter the Sacred Mosque with complete peace in a way that you will shave your heads and have hair-cuts; you will have no fear. It was only that God knew what you did not; so, before this, He blessed you with a victory near at hand. (48:27)

Departure for Makkah

- 1400-1500 faithful believers departed for Makkah in Dhul Qadaah 6th Hijri with 70 camels taken for sacrifice (as per the law of Umrah).
- They put on the Ihram at Dhul Al Halifah near Makkah before the Haram.
- One companion was sent forward to check for signs of an enemy ambush.

- He informed the Prophet that Quraysh was misinterpreting this journey, and they thought that the Muslims were coming for a war.
- They had also posted a few armed men at the entry points to Makkah.
- The Prophet felt sad to hear that, as he had come only to fulfill God's command, as shown in the dream, but apparently Quraysh was not ready to heed what had already happened to them.
- These sentiments expressed his love and kinship for his tribesmen and his frustration with the Quraysh's uncompromising nature.

What is Umrah?

- Umrah can be done at any time of the year.
- It is called Hajj-e-Asghar (Minor Hajj).
- All its rituals are performed within Kabaah and the person does not need to travel anywhere like in Hajj.
- The person must wear the Ihram before entering the bounds of Haram.
- You can bring animals for sacrifice, but it is not required.

Haram and Ihram

- This is Haram, not Haraam (means prohibited). Haram is a sacred area around Kabaah where certain otherwise permissible activities become prohibited.
- From the time of Prophet Ibrahim, a designated area around the Kabaah, considered sacred, is called the Haram.
- No fighting, killing, or even hunting is allowed in this area.
- Ihram is a white piece of cloth. When you are in the state of Ihram for Umrah or Hajj, even certain permissible acts become prohibited, like cutting your hair, etc.

What is considered *Haram*

- The Haram is the sacred boundary of Makkah within which certain acts are considered unlawful, which may be lawful elsewhere. It is prohibited to hunt wild animals, damage any plant or tree, graze animals, carry weapons, or fight or behave in a manner that will violate the sanctity of **Masjid al-Haraam**.

Approximate boundary of Haram

Approximate boundary of Haram

Entry in the Bounds of Haram

- The Prophet, after consulting his companions, took another route to enter the Haram, reaching the plains of Hudaybiyah.

- This strategy worked, and Muslims were able to enter the Haram safely without encountering Quraysh.

- It is reported that the she-camel of the Prophet, al Qaswa, stopped at a place in Hudaybiyah and refused to move forward, which the Prophet took as a sign that God wanted them to stop here.

- The Quraysh first reached Asfan to face the Muslim caravan, but later turned toward Hudaybiyah.

- The Prophet stayed in Hudaybiyah, believing that God did not want him to leave this place and that he should remain within the sanctity of the Haram to avoid war.

- He wanted to make this journey as peaceful as possible, keeping the sanctity of Umrah.

Reaching out to Quraysh

- A delegation of a few friendly people from Makkah, from the tribe of Banu Khuzaah, met the Prophet in Hudaybiyah, and the Prophet informed them of his intention to perform Umrah. They told the Prophet that Quraysh would prefer to die before they allowed Muslims to enter Makkah.

- He told them if Quraysh agrees on a period when they would not interfere between the Prophet and the people living in Arabia, then he is ready to compromise, but if they insist on war, then the Muslims are ready to fight – the Prophet was asking for a time duration when he could reach out to the people of Arabia and introduce Islam to them in a peaceful environment instead of constantly fighting wars with Quraysh.

- When the delegation returned to Quraysh, they hesitantly agreed to the proposal and began negotiating.

- The Prophet chose his companion and son-in-law, Uthman bin Affan, for this task, and he left for Makkah.

- Since Quraysh had the intention to put more pressure on Muslims, they delayed the negotiation talks and spread the rumors that Uthman had been killed. This rumor was intended to frighten Muslims in this situation, to get a more favorable deal for them.

The Pledge of Ridwan

- Contrary to what Quraysh was thinking, the Muslims got enraged when they heard the fake news of the murder of Uthman.

- The Prophet sat down under a tree and took an oath from every Muslim that he would not leave this place without avenging the unjust killing of Uthman.

- This turn of events prompted Quraysh to adopt a more reasonable attitude, and they sent Uthman back to his camp, along with a few people, to negotiate the deal in front of the Prophet Muhammad.

- God was very pleased with the loyalty and commitment of the Muslims who pledged to support Prophet Muhammad at any cost with a few arms.

- The only true asset and power the Muslims had during this pledge were their firm belief in God and His Messenger, and a strong sense of certainty in His help and support for the believers.

- This pledge, known as the **Pledge of Ridwan** (the Pledge of God's Pleasure), is a sign of strong belief and commitment to God. These Muslims got special status in Muslim society and in the eyes of God.

The Agreement for Peace

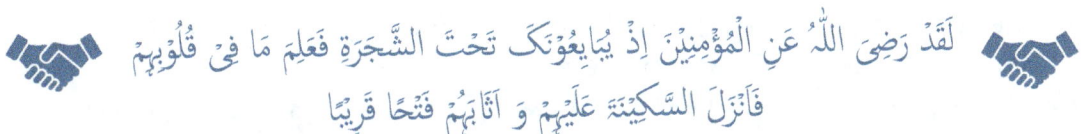

لَقَدْ رَضِيَ اللّٰهُ عَنِ الْمُؤْمِنِينَ إِذْ يُبَايِعُوْنَكَ تَحْتَ الشَّجَرَةِ فَعَلِمَ مَا فِىْ قُلُوْبِهِمْ فَأَنْزَلَ السَّكِيْنَةَ عَلَيْهِمْ وَ أَثَابَهُمْ فَتْحًا قَرِيْبًا

"God is pleased with the believers when they pledge allegiance to you under the tree: He knew what was in their hearts, and He sent down peace of reassurance on them, and He rewarded them with Victory that appears. (48:18)

The Quraysh refused to refer to Muhammad as a Prophet when drafting the agreement. The following agreement was written between Muhammad bin Abdullah and Sohail bin Amr:

- They have agreed to remove the danger of war for ten years. During this period, the people will live in peace, and both parties will refrain from attacking each other.
- Any person from the Quraysh who goes to Muhammad without permission from his tribe or guardian will be returned, and any person from the companions of Muhammad who goes to the Quraysh will not be returned.
- All kinds of hostile activities will remain suspended. Neither will go against the other, either openly or in secret.
- Anyone else who wishes to side with Muhammad and enter into this agreement can do so, and anyone who wishes to side with the Quraysh and enter into the agreement can do so.
- You (Muhammad) shall return this year and shall not enter Makkah, but next year, we (Quraysh) will not block you, and you can enter Makkah with your companions. You will stay there for three days and possess the soldier's arms (swords in their sheaths). You will not carry any other arms into the city.

Witnesses:
- From the Muslim side, Abu Bakr, Umar, Uthman, Saad Bin Abi Waqas, and Muhammad bin Maslamah. From the Quraysh side, Huwaytab bin Abd al Uzzah, Makraz bin Hafs.

The Unhappy Muslims

- Anyone who reads this agreement can tell that it is one-sided and demonstrates the upper hand of the Quraysh.
- The Muslims felt humiliated as they were not allowed to perform Umrah.
- Omar got impatient and asked the Prophet, "*Are we not on the side of the Truth and Quraysh on the side of falsehood?*". The Prophet responded, *"Certainly!"* After some debate, the Prophet told Omar, "*I am the Prophet of God, and God will not waste my efforts and not let Muslims down.*"
- The Prophet promised that for the person who would be returned to the Quraysh in case he escapes to Medina and wants to join the Muslims, God would find a way out for him/her.
- As it was not possible to perform Umrah this year, Muslims slaughtered the sacrificial animals that they brought with them, shaved their heads, and took off their Ihram as per the instructions given by God.
- It is important to note that Muslims brought sacrificial animals with them which was a sign that they had no intention to fight but Quraish made excuses to deny Umrah to Muslims.
- It is reported that the Muslims were reluctant to slaughter the animals. Still, the Prophet's wife, Umm Salamah, suggested that the Prophet perform the sacrifice of his animal.
- When the Muslims saw that, they started following his example and sacrificed their animals.
- On the way back, Muslims had a few thoughts in their minds:

  - What was the purpose of that journey?
  - What did they gain, and was there any benefit in this journey?
  - If they had already pledged to fight, why did they agree on a one-sided truce?
  - The dreams of the Prophet are always true, but what about this one?

Revelation of Surah Fath

إِنَّا فَتَحْنَا لَكَ فَتْحًا مُّبِينًا

There is no doubt (O Prophet) that We have given you a
clear and open Victory (Surah Fath:1)

- God knows what's in our hearts and minds. He was listening to all the doubts that Muslims had in their minds, and He responded to them and honored their commitment to God and His Messenger.
- God revealed Surah Fath of the Quran during the journey back to Medina, and it was a blessing for the Muslims, bringing them peace and tranquility in their hearts and removing all their doubts.
- Umar ibn al-Khattab reported: The Messenger of Allah said, "A Surah has been revealed to me tonight that is more beloved to me than everything over which the sun rises." Then, the Prophet recited verse 1 of Surah Fath.

God explained the Agreement

A) The Dream

- God told the Muslims that the opportunity to perform Umrah would come, and Muslims would enter Makkah with such honor and peace that they would face no danger from anywhere – a promise that has been delayed to fulfill for a reason.

B) Protection from Battle

- Fighting within the boundaries of Haram would have started negative propaganda against Muslims, who always talked about the sanctity of the House of God. This would have resulted in mixed feelings towards the Muslims and the Quraysh. But now everyone was blaming Quraysh for a hostile attitude against a people who merely came to perform a religious obligation.
- Many Muslims in Makkah were hiding their Islam. As a result of the fighting, it would have caused great harm to those Muslims who were waiting for the right opportunity to migrate.
- Many people living in Makkah were unhappy with their leaders, and their hearts were convinced of Islam, but they were unable to make any decision (Khalid bin Walid, Amr bin Al-Aas, Muawiyyah bin Abi Sufyan, all of whom later became famous Muslims).

C) A Clear Victory

- A hostile enemy like Quraysh's acceptance of a truce for ten years was a sign of weakness on their side.
- Allowing Muslims next year for Umrah suggests that they accept the right of Muslims to the Kabaah also.
- The truce will remove Quraysh as a party if Muslims want to extend their reach and communication to other neighboring tribes.
- This would also allow other tribes to see the beauty of Islam firsthand without the danger of reprisal from Quraysh – for example, right after this, Banu Khuzaah signed a friendship agreement with Muslims.
- It allowed Muslims to act against those enemies who were conspiring against Muslims due to the support from Quraysh.

D) The matter of returning Muslims to Quraysh

- Islam is the name of an ideology and faith in the heart first before anything else. People who have accepted Islam can continue to remain in Makkah for now until Muslims gain power. God even allowed them to hide their Islam if required, until it became easier for them to practice it.
- Also, they can settle elsewhere than Medina if Muslims can make friendship agreements with more tribes.
- The agreement did not apply to women, and they will be protected in Medina.

Lesson for us

- God is the best Planner, but sometimes, we cannot understand the wisdom behind His Plans and actions. He designs and fashions His Plans.
- The Treaty of Hudaybiyah seemed one-sided in favor of Quraysh, but it began to yield benefits to the Muslims immediately. Such events showed that God remained with His Messenger and guided him throughout the mission. It also showed the unwavering trust that the Prophet had in God.

Why do you think a peaceful environment created as a result of a treaty was good for Islam and Muslims?

The Fashioner / Designer

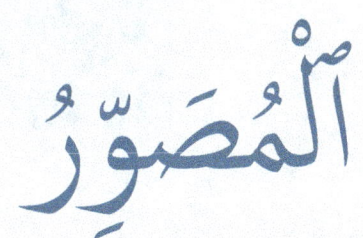

- God calls Himself Al Musawwir, which means the one who fashions, draws, or designs something, and He is the Best Designer.
- He designs His plans also in the best possible way, as we will see the benefits of the Treaty of Hudaybiyah.
- The Quran states that when He created us as human beings, He fashioned us in the best possible way.
- Al Musawwir is closely related to Al Khaliq, meaning the Creator – He did not just create everything, but also fashioned it with the best design, as evidenced by the beauty of the world around us.

هُوَ اللّٰهُ الْخَالِقُ الْبَارِئُ الْمُصَوِّرُ

He is Allah who is the Creator, the Originator and the Fashioner (Surah Hashr:24)

- In this verse, all three attributes of God are related to each other.
- God gifted that talent to human beings, and we also have architects, artists, and designers among us.

Chapter 13

Fruits of the Treaty of Hudaybiyah

In this chapter, we will learn about the benefits and fruits that the Treaty of Hudaybiyah displayed, which no one was expecting.

Significant results of the Treaty

- The Treaty of Hudaybiyah was the first time the Quraysh and the Prophet signed an agreement on equal footing. And this demonstrates that the Muslims were not only gaining their due respect, but eventually, they will gain the upper hand.
- The Quraysh leaders also realized that the tide was turning. And that was the primary reason they did not allow Muslims to perform Umrah that year, just to show the Arabs that they still have an upper hand.

1. The Victory of Khayber

- All the Jews who were exiled from Medina settled in Khayber and its neighborhood, and their population grew significantly.
- The Jews did not stop plotting against Muslims through backdoor tactics.
- Due to this, God instructed the Prophet and the Muslims to attack Khayber and permanently eliminate the influence of the Jews in this area.
- However, God did not allow anyone who did not come along on the Hudaybiyah journey to participate in this attack; as God had promised the believers, only those who took the pledge of Ridwan received a great deal of war booty.
- Jews could not get any help from Quraysh due to the Treaty of Hudaybiyah.
- Their large and strong fortresses and castles were seized, and the Jews were defeated big-time.
- They requested the Prophet for peace, and he agreed on the following condition: Muslims would possess all their property, land, and wealth, but the Jews would continue to work on the agricultural land as farmers, and half of the produce would go to the Muslims – a punishment was given to them for constantly conspiring against the Muslims.

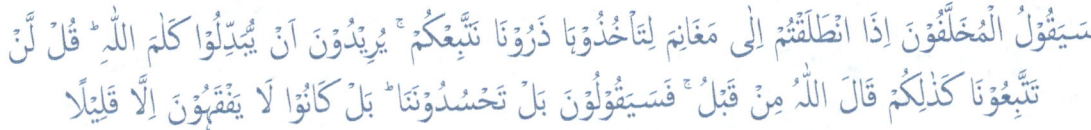

"Those who lagged [will say], when you are going to march to take the booty [in war]: "Allow us to follow you." They wish to change God's decree: Say: "You will not follow us: God has already declared this beforehand": then they will say: "But you are jealous of us." No, but little do they understand [such things]."
(Surah Fath:15)

2. The Umrah

- As per the Treaty, the Prophet decided to perform the Umrah exactly one year after it was signed.
- More people were able to join this time as the number of believers continued to increase.

- As a precaution, the Muslims took one sword per person but left them outside of the Haram to maintain its sanctity and assigned a 200-man group to guard it (they took turns to do the Umrah).
- The Quraysh left Makkah for three days as per the Treaty, and the Muslims performed Umrah in a peaceful environment.
- After performing the animal sacrifices, the Muslims left Makkah as per the deal.
- The Umrah was performed as per the Prophet's dream in a very peaceful environment.

3. The Sons of Quraysh accepted Islam

- During this peaceful time, many young people from the Quraysh started pondering on the Message of Islam, the help that had come to the Muslims, and their ever-growing influence.
- They became convinced that Islam is a true religion of God, and their forefathers had invented these idols.

- Two great leaders from Quraysh who played a pivotal role in the history of Islam, Khalid bin Walid and Amr bin Al Aas, came to the Prophet and accepted Islam.
- Similarly, Uthman bin Talha and Muawiyyah bin Abi Sufyan also came to Medina and accepted Islam.
- None of them was under the protection or guardianship of any of the leaders of Quraysh, so they were not returned to Makkah (as the Treaty clause applied only to those with a guardian or protector in Makkah), but those who came were all young leaders of Quraysh.

Every child is born with his/her nature (Islam). This is his/her parents who make him/her a Jew, a Christian, or a Zoroastrian. (Sahih Al Bukhari #1292)

4. Call to Faith and Acceptance

- Muslims went to far places in groups to deliver the message of Islam, and Islam spread in the surrounding areas during this time of peace like never before.

- Some of the tribes sent their delegations to meet the Prophet and realized immediately that he was a true Prophet.

- Some people came to learn about Islam on their own, then returned to teach it to their tribesmen, while others preferred to stay in Medinah – Abu Hurairah was one of them.

- It is reported in history that 1,500 people went for the Umrah at the time of the Treaty of Hudaybiyah, and 10,000 people went to Makkah at the time of the Conquest of Makkah (which occurred three years later, and not everyone went to Makkah) – that shows the number of people who accepted Islam in this period of peace.

- The following tribes expressed their loyalty towards the Muslims during this time: Banu Saad Bin Bakr, Mazinah, Abd Al Qays, Tay (the tribe of Hatim Tai), Banu Tamim, Banu Azd, and Banu Kindah.

Muslims projected to be fastest-growing major religious group

Estimated percent change in population size, 2015-2060

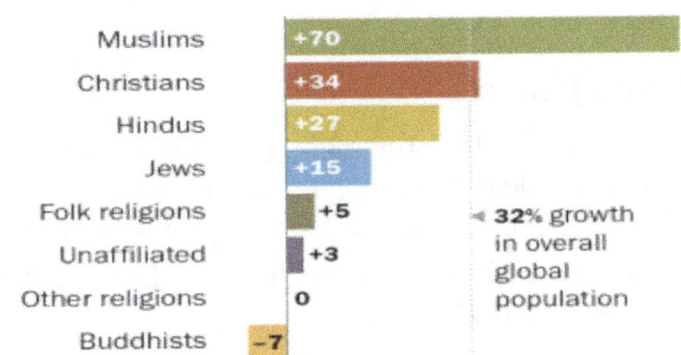

Muslims	+70
Christians	+34
Hindus	+27
Jews	+15
Folk religions	+5
Unaffiliated	+3
Other religions	0
Buddhists	-7

◄ 32% growth in overall global population

Source: Pew Research Center demographic projections. See Methodology for details.
"The Changing Global Religious Landscape"

PEW RESEARCH CENTER

Incident of Adi Bin Hatim accepting Islam

- Adi Bin Hatim was the son of Hatim Tai and the influential king of the Tay tribe.
- His sister was captured when Muslims raided their region, but the Prophet set her free and gave her gifts and an animal to transport her to Syria, where Adi fled due to the attack – the sister told him about the kindness of the Prophet and introduced the Prophet as the King of Medina.
- Adi came to Medina and met the Prophet. The Prophet invited him to his house, but on the way, a poor old woman stopped the Prophet for a need, and the Prophet listened to her carefully and fulfilled her request.
- Adi thought that if a person paid so much attention to a poor lady, he could not be a king, but a Prophet.
- When they entered the Prophet's house, the Prophet spread out a cushion for himself, and he sat on the floor. This kind gesture impressed Adi.
- Then the Prophet asked him if he belonged to a specific sect of Christianity and took one-fourth of the war booty from his people as their leader, knowing that this is not allowed in Christianity – Adi was amazed because ordinary people would not know about this.
- Then the Prophet told him:

"Perhaps the poverty of my companions, the large number of their enemies, and their lesser number are stopping you from entering my faith. Remember that soon, these people shall possess so much wealth that they will want to give it away, but no one will take it. You think that the rule will always belong to others, but remember that the white palaces of Babylon will be under the Muslims very soon."

5. The Battle of Mautah

- At this peaceful time, the Prophet wanted to pay attention to Northern Arabia, where Christians and Jews had significant influence – he sent a letter to the governor of Rome, based in Basrah, through his envoy, Harith bin Umayr.
- He was killed by one of the Ghassanid leaders, Sharjeel bin Amr, in the city of Mautah (now in southern Jordan).
- The Prophet sent an army of 3000 men led by Zayd bin Harithah and gave instructions that the following people should lead the army if Zayd were martyred:
  - Jafar bin Abi Talib
  - Abdullah bin Rawahah

- The Muslim army encountered a massive Roman army when they reached the area.
- First, they decided to retreat and consult with the Prophet about this situation, but then they decided to fight – all three leaders got martyred one after the other.
- Khalid bin Walid took command of the army and fought bravely against the enemy – it is said that nine swords broke in his hands, inflicting heavy losses on the Roman army.
- Finally, the Romans retreated, but the Muslims did not have enough people to take over the city in the presence of a large army.
- When the Muslim army returned, the Prophet greeted them and bestowed the title "Saifullah" (the sword of God) on Khalid bin Walid.

If you must tell your non-Muslim friend about Islam in 1 minute, what would that be?

Lessons for us

- Many Western scholars have tried to make a point that Islam was spread through the sword, but if we look at the history of Islam closely, it will be clear to us that Islam has always spread in times of peace.
- After the treaty, it was the first time that Muslims and pagans started to engage in buying, selling, traveling, and all other social aspects of life. The Message of Islam was made known to every tribe of the Arabian Peninsula through such activities.
- However, this could not have been possible without the Muslims, who, taking advantage of the peaceful environment, made efforts to spread the message of Islam, and the nonbelievers, after having assessed the lifestyle of the Muslims at a close range, recognized and accepted the truth of Islam.
- This is exactly how Islam reached many countries like Malaysia and Indonesia, where some Muslim traders went for trading.
- We need peace in the world to make people aware of Islam.

The Generous Extender

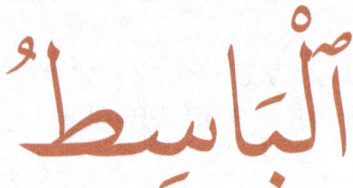

- Allah did not use this attribute as one of His names in the Quran, but He made references to it by saying that He extends people's provisions (or anything) generously.
- This generous or gracious extension of any good can also be seen as a blessing from Allah.
- This is also used in the context of making things easy for someone – for example, from the state of poverty to richness or from trouble to ease, etc.
- Similarly, Allah extended the blessings of Islam to many people after the Treaty of Hudaybiyah and continues to do so to this day.
- Of course, for someone to benefit from these blessings, they should make the intention and put in the effort before they receive them.
- Most people restrict the meaning of Rizq (Provisions) to food only but it is a very wide word that encompasses anything good that we receive from Allah including Islam, our parents, children etc.

Allah extends the provision (material and other good) for whom He wills and restricts [for who He wills]. (Surah Rad:26)

SURAH KAHAF REALITY CHALLENGE

Musa (AS) embarked on a journey with a man of knowledge, and during this journey, the man did some things that Musa (AS) did not approve of because he was unaware of the reality behind them. Read Surah Kahaf and all the story of Musa and Khidr and write down the reality behind each incident.

Action	Reality
Man broke the boat of a poor sailor	
Man killed an innocent child	
Man helped repair a falling wall in a town whose people were rude	

Chapter 14

Letters to the Rulers of Different Countries

In this chapter, we will learn about the letters that Prophet Muhammad wrote to the leaders of various regions and countries before the final punishment was inflicted on the disbelievers.

Prophet Muhammad is sent to the entire world

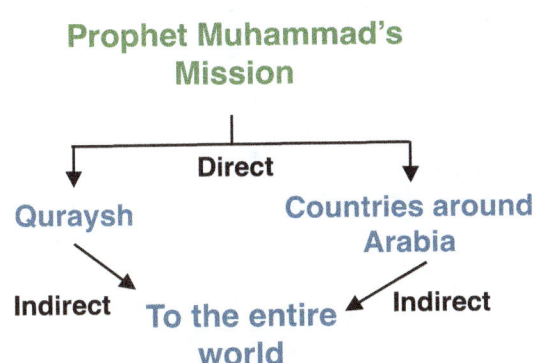

- The Quran was revealed in the language of the Quraysh, and the Prophet was asked to teach Islam to them directly.
- But at the same time, he was gradually asked to reach out to other tribes, people in the area, and, finally, to other countries and states around Arabia.
- This is the practice of God: at times, instead of sending Prophets and Messengers to each city or town, He sends them to the center of civilization, and then it spreads out from that center.
- For Arabs and surrounding pagans, Makkah was the hub of all activities.
- God told the Prophet that His religion (Islam) would gain dominance over other faiths, whether people like it or not.
- The predictions were made in the previous divine scriptures (Bible) that the last Prophet will be sent for the entire humanity, and Islam will be the only God-sent religion until the Day of Judgment.

وَ مَآ اَرْسَلْنٰکَ اِلَّا رَحْمَةً لِّلْعٰلَمِیْنَ

We have sent you not but as a mercy for all the Worlds."
(Anbiya:107)

وَ مَآ اَرْسَلْنٰکَ اِلَّا کَآفَّةً لِّلنَّاسِ بَشِیْرًا وَّ نَذِیْرًا وَّ لٰکِنَّ اَکْثَرَ النَّاسِ لَا یَعْلَمُوْنَ

We have not sent you but as a universal [messenger] to men, giving them glad tidings, and warning them [against sin], but most men understand not." (Saba:28)

Invitation to Foreign Kings

- God has said in the Quran about the relationship between Prophet Muhammad, Muslims, and the rest of the world. The Children of Ismail were made the middle nation to pass this message on to the world.

وَ كَذَلِكَ جَعَلْنَكُمْ أُمَّةً وَّسَطًا لِّتَكُونُوا شُهَدَآءَ عَلَى النَّاسِ وَ يَكُونَ الرَّسُولُ عَلَيْكُمْ شَهِيدًا

Thus, similarly, We have made you (Muslims) **a middle nation**, that you might be a witness over other nations, and the Messenger is a witness over yourselves. (Baqarah:143)

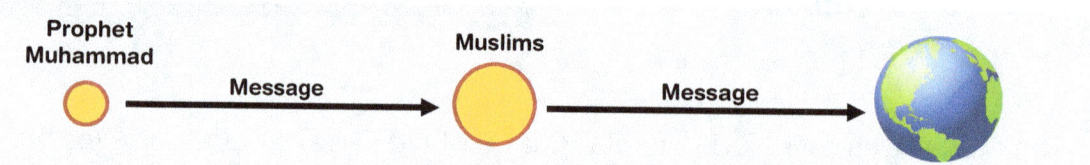

"The progeny of Ibrahim would be the owners of the gates, and all forces in the world will gain blessings through his generations." (Bible-Genesis, 22:18)

"He would be such a supporter who would stay with people until the world's end." (Bible-John:14:16)

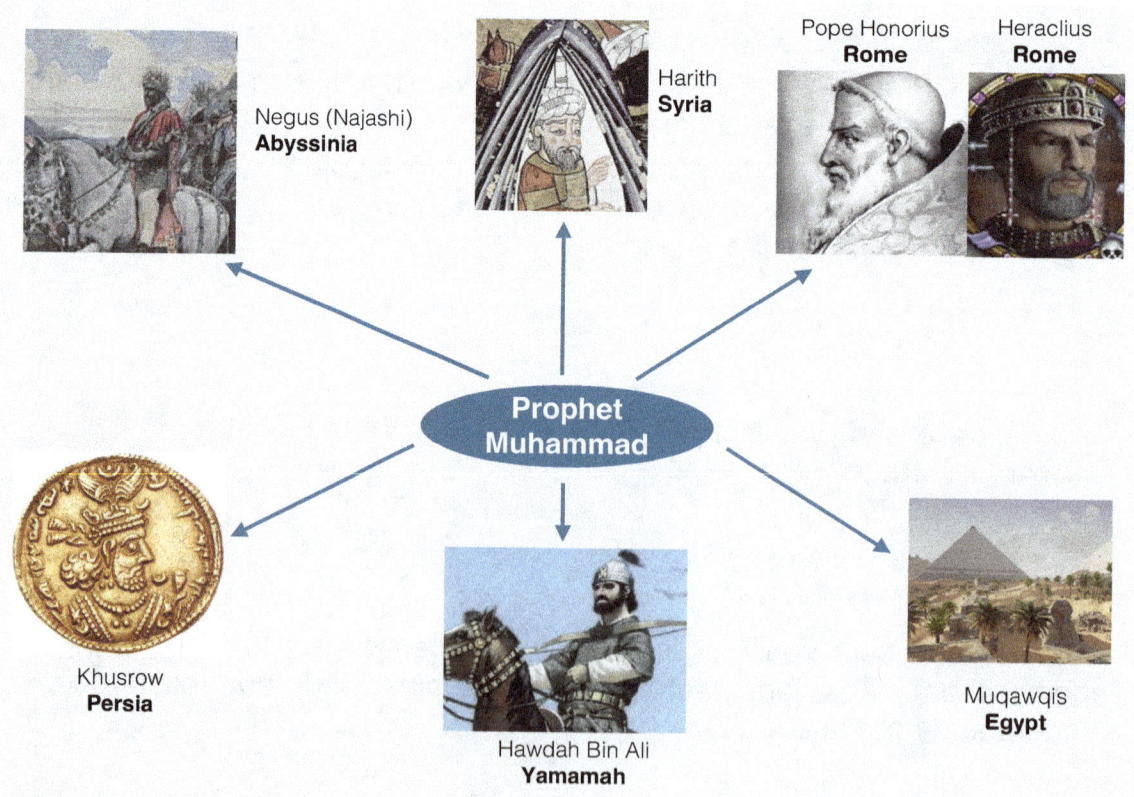

The Geographical Map

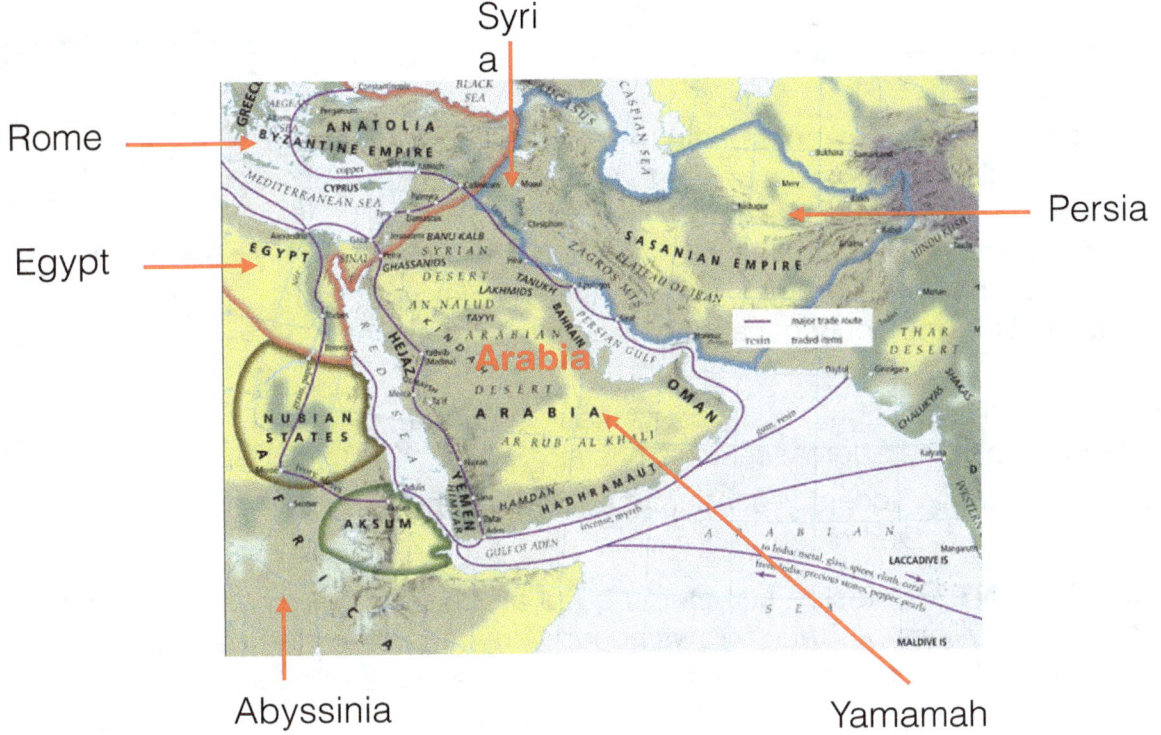

Syria

Rome

Persia

Egypt

Abyssinia

Yamamah

- All these rulers, kings, and governors were very well aware of the events and struggles between Muslims, Quraysh, and Jews.
- They also observed the recent victories that Muslims had achieved. Like Jews and Christians near Medina, they also knew that a final Prophet was about to come to this region.
- Receiving a letter from Prophet Muhammad was not a surprise for them.
- However, as rulers of a country, they found it difficult to accept another's authority and to relinquish their people's religion, as religion played a critical role at the time.
- The ruler's religion is the religion of everyone in that state.

Content of the Letters

- The core beliefs explained in the Quran are Monotheism, Prophethood, Accountability, and the Hereafter.
- This serves as a reminder of the responsibilities they had as rulers of these nations. If they decide to remain on the path of falsehood, then their people will also remain deprived of the true faith of Islam. They will bear the burden of the sins of all the people of their nation who could not accept the truth because of them.
- Clarified the real figure of Jesus as the true Prophet of God in case the addressee is a Christian.
- An invitation to accept Prophet Muhammad as the last Messenger of God on earth.

Letters

IMPORTANT: If you start something good and beneficial, you will receive the reward, as will anyone who follows you. If you start something bad or useless, you will receive a bad deed for it, as well as for anyone who follows you.

Responses from the Leaders

- They all responded differently depending on the situation and the strength of their willpower.
- However, it is important to note that they were all aware of the Prophet and wanted to know more about him.

Abyssinia (Najashi) **Accepted Islam**	First, he declined with an apology, stating that he does not have the support in the country. When the Prophet later sent him another letter, he kissed it and placed it on his head as a sign of respect.
Rome (Heraclius) **Convinced but could not accept Islam**	He asked many questions of Abu Sufyan, the leader of the Quraysh, who happened to be in his land when the letter was written. He was very impressed, but he could not find the courage to accept Islam due to the fear of revolt from courtiers and religious leaders

Rome (Pope Honorius) **Not known if he was convinced**	The Pope read the letter in the Church and testified to its authenticity, stating that it came from a Prophet. His listeners became so infuriated that they beat him to death. It is not proven if he accepted Prophet Muhammad as the true Prophet.
Egypt (Muqawqis) **Did not Accept Islam**	He honored the messenger who brought him the letter and sent many gifts back to the Prophet, but did not express any desire to accept Islam, nor did he do so later. It seems that he also did not find the courage to face his ministers and religious leaders.
Persia (Khusrow) **Did not Accept Islam**	He became furious, tore up the letter, and shouted: "How could our servant possess such courage to write such a letter to us?" When the Prophet heard about it, he said: "his kingdom will be ripped in the same way in which he tore up my letter."
Yamamah (Hawdah) **Accepted Islam conditionally**	He accepted Islam on the condition that the Prophet would include him in his government, and he would remain the governor of Yamamah. The Prophet did not accept the condition, but soon afterward, Hawdah died.
Syria (Harith) **Did not Accept Islam**	The Prophet sent him a letter stating that if he accepted Islam, he could remain the leader of his nation. He became angry and said no one dared to look at his country with bad intentions. The Prophet predicted that his reign would end soon. In 14 AH, when Muslims took over Syria, they ended a 500-year-old state.

What were the main reasons that stopped leaders and kings from accepting the truth or changing religions even if they knew it was true?

Kings of Byzantine and Persia

Dialogue between Heraclius and Abu Sufyan

Heraclius

Abu Sufyan

Heraclius	Abu Sufyan
What is the status of this person in your community?	He has a high status and belongs to a noble family
Has there been a king among his ancestors?	No!
Have you ever accused him of any falsehood before this?	Never!
Do his followers include the weak or the nation's leaders?	They are all weak people
Are his followers increasing or decreasing?	They are increasing
Has anyone left their religion after entering once?	Never!
Have you ever fought a battle with him, and what was the result?	He has harmed us, and so have we
Does he break his promises?	No, but we are in a period of peace; nothing can be said
Has anyone claimed prophethood before this?	No!

- Heraclius also asked about Islam's teachings.
- Heraclius told Abu Sufyan that if he was telling the truth, then these were all the signs of a true prophet.
- He knew that a final prophet was about to come, but was not sure when and where.
- He also told Abu Sufyan that had he been there, he would have washed his (Prophet's) feet (a symbol of reverence).
- While Heraclius was acknowledging this, his courtiers became furious.
- When he saw that the situation was becoming serious, he made an excuse that he was testing their faithfulness in Christianity and wanted to see their reaction.
- He was a wise man who recognized the Prophet, but he dared not face his nation.

Khusrow – The King of Persia

- Khusrow became very upset and asked Badhan, the governor of Yemen, to arrest "the Arab who claimed to be the Prophet" and present him in court.
- Badhan sent his people to Medinah, who read out the governor's order and told them that if the order were not obeyed, Khusrow would destroy their country.

- The Prophet asked them to return since Khusrow had already been killed by his son, Shirawayh. "Tell your master that the Islamic rule will soon reach him."
- When Badhan's people returned, he received news from Persia that Khusrow had been killed because of his excessively oppressive ways and that now, no hostility should be adopted towards the Prophet of Arabia.
- Badhan came to believe that Prophet Muhammad was a messenger of God, and God informed him about this incident from a faraway place
- He accepted Islam immediately.
- There were incidents in the life of the Prophet Muhammad when God revealed to him certain current and future events. These incidents were among the miracles the Prophet showed to the people around him.

Lesson for us

- The Prophet's letters were short, crisp, and to the point. Historians told us that they were all written in a single paragraph. He began every letter with the name of God. He also addressed the leaders with due respect. Even though the main message was the same, each letter was tailored to the person it was addressed to to show them the respect they expected.

The Witness
(over all things)

- Allah calls Himself Al-Shaheed, who is a Witness over everything because He knows everything, and He sees everything, whether done openly or in hiding. In other words He is also All-Observing.

- One aspect of Al-Shaheed is that Allah is watching and will hold us accountable on that Day, like a witness is presented in the court when someone is prosecuted.

- No one can escape His Judgment.

- Scholars often argue that understanding this name should transform a person's character, both in secret and in public.

- Knowing Allah is Ash-Shaheed develops a constant awareness of Allah (**Taqwa**), as He sees every deed and will testify for or against the servant.

- He witnessed how the Kings of all those nations responded to the invitation of Prophet Muhammad towards the Truth, and they will be judged according to their intention and what's in their hearts.

وَ لِكُلٍّ جَعَلْنَا مَوَالِيَ مِمَّا تَرَكَ الْوَالِدٰنِ وَ الْأَقْرَبُوْنَ ۖ وَ الَّذِيْنَ عَقَدَتْ اَيْمَانُكُمْ فَاٰتُوْهُمْ نَصِيْبَهُمْ ۚ اِنَّ اللّٰهَ كَانَ عَلٰى كُلِّ شَىْءٍ شَهِيْدًا

[Precisely these preferences are kept in consideration in the distribution of inheritance as well] and in the wealth left by parents and relatives, We have appointed heirs for each [according to these preferences; do not try to change them]. As for those with whom you have entered into agreements, give them their share. [However, in this regard, there should be no intention of harming an heir] because God is witness over all things. (4:33)

SEERAH ACTIVITY

HANDWRITE A LETTER

"Handwrite a Letter" to the **King or Queen of Wonderland**, who is still a non-Muslim, and you want him/her and his/her people to accept Islam.

Instructions

- The letter should be handwritten.
- Be respectful and to the point.
- Going to war is not an option, because this authority was given only to a Messenger.
- You have to convince him/her to come to Islam by showing the truth and benefits of Islam in this world and in the Hereafter.
- The letter should be between 200 and 300 words.

Chapter 15

Cancellation of the Treaty of Hudaybiyah

In this chapter, we will learn why Prophet Muhammad had to cancel the Treaty of Hudaybiyah and the consequences that disbelievers face as a result.

Cancellation of the Treaty

Violation of the Agreement by the Quraysh

- The Treaty of Hudaybiyah allowed both the Muslims and the Quraysh to form alliances with whomever they chose. All new parties will become part of the Treaty of Hudaybiyah as soon as they enter a partnership with any of the main parties.

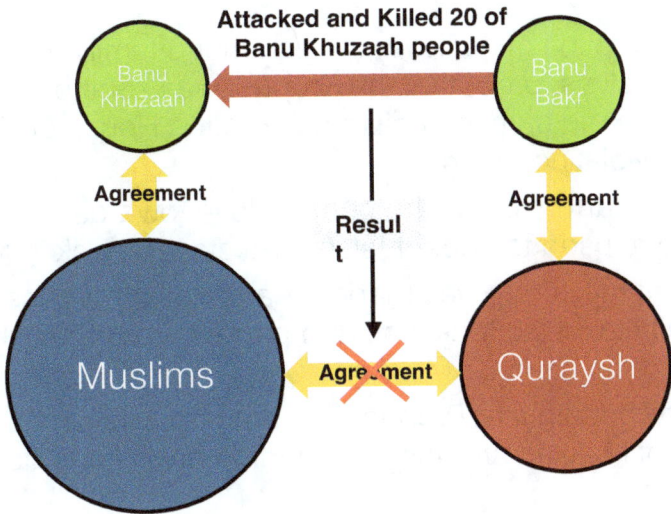

- Muslims made an alliance with Banu Khuzaah, while Quraysh made an alliance with Banu Bakr.
- Some leaders among the Quraysh were not happy at the time of the Treaty.
- Banu Khuzaah and Banu Bakr had a history of enmity, and those Qurayshi leaders saw this as an opportunity to sabotage the Treaty.
- They incited Banu Bakr to an attack to teach Banu Khuzaah a lesson for siding with the Muslims.
- Twenty people from Banu Khuzaah were killed, and they were forced to take refuge inside the Haram, thinking that they would be safe.
- Banu Bakr violated the sanctity of the Haram while encouraged by the Quraysh and continued to attack Banu Khuzaah.
- This was an open violation of the Treaty by the Quraysh and their allies, thinking that Muslims would have a softer reaction due to the Treaty.

Quraysh tried to make amends

- The Quraysh soon realized the severity of the situation and sent Abu Sufyan to apologize to the Prophet and request that the Treaty be continued. Abu Sufyan used Abu Bakr, Omar, and Ali to convince the Prophet to uphold the agreement.
- However, the Prophet disagreed, as instructed by God, for the following reasons:
  - Due to the resumption of social activities among family members on both sides, these Muslims forgot that the Prophet was sent to bring the Abrahamic message of monotheism back to the House of God, and idolaters were violating that right.
  - These Muslims started to feel the bond of love towards the family members who refused to accept Islam and stayed back in Makkah.
  - They forgot that the Treaty was made for a specific purpose – to give time and opportunity to all the Makkans and people around Makkah to listen to the message of the Quran.
  - They started forgetting that Prophet Muhammad was sent as a Messenger to the people of Makkah and the surrounding areas, and he had a duty to fulfill.

The Cancellation of the Treaty violating the agreement and gaining time.

- God gave the following instructions to the Prophet and Muslims regarding the Treaty and other agreements that the Prophet had made with Quraysh and other tribes around Medina.
- All those agreements with the idolator that lack a time limit will be considered canceled after 4 months.
- Any time-bound agreement that the idolators failed to honor will be considered canceled after 4 months.
- Any time-bound agreement (for example, 1 year) that the idolators have honored will come to an end; thereafter, no new deal will be signed.
- Due to the sanctity of the Treaty of Hudaybiyah, because it was done in Haram, the Muslims were bound to honor it until the Quraysh violated it – now the Muslims have no responsibility to honor it.
- At the end of all agreements, the Muslims will be considered in a state of war with the Quraysh and idolaters until they believe, offer Salah, and pay Zakah (required by every Muslim in that situation to prove to the state that they were Muslims).
- Everyone still has the opportunity to listen to the Quran and learn about Islam.
- This annulment of all agreements and the final warning will be given during the next Hajj, so everyone knows about it.

The Watcher
(Overseer)

- Allah is the Watcher and Overseer over His creations and their affairs – He did not just create and leave everyone to do whatever they want to do.
- This attribute also means that Allah does not allow any good or bad to occur that can go unnoticed, regardless of how small or large it is.
- This attribute also refers to Allah as a Guard who protects things that must be protected.
- Quraish leaders did not realize that Allah is watching their actions, and any direct or indirect violation of the treaty will be considered a breach, and they will have to bear the consequences of it.
- God also called the Quran Muhaymin because it guards the Message of God and keeps a watch over all the Books of God that He has sent (for example Bible, Torah, etc.) – meaning if we find some teachings of God in the Bible or Torah, we must verify if that teaching is given in the Quran or not or at least not against the teachings of the Quran.

هُوَ اللَّهُ الَّذِى لَآ اِلَٰهَ اِلَّا هُوَ ٱلْمَلِكُ ٱلْقُدُّوسُ ٱلسَّلَٰمُ ٱلْمُؤْمِنُ
ٱلْمُهَيْمِنُ ٱلْعَزِيزُ ٱلْجَبَّارُ ٱلْمُتَكَبِّرُ ۚ سُبْحَٰنَ ٱللَّهِ عَمَّا يُشْرِكُونَ

He is the very God besides whom there is no deity, the Sovereign Lord, the Holy, the Embodiment of Peace, the Giver of Tranquillity, the Watcher Guardian, the Mighty, the Extremely Powerful, the Most High; exalted is God above what they state as partners! (59:23)

Why did God not allow Muslims to break the contracts that had a time limit (for example, no war for 1 year) to punish them?

Chapter 16

The Opening of Makkah

In this chapter, we will cover the Opening of Makkah for true Islam that changed Islam's future forever, and we are still seeing the fruits of that victory to this day.

The Objective of Prophet's Mission

Bringing people back to worshiping only <u>ONE True God who created this Universe</u> is the ultimate goal of every Prophet and Messenger.

- The Opening of Makkah for Islam is the most significant and glorious event in the history of Islam.
- The main objective that was given to the Prophet and his companions after the migration had two parts:
  - Purify the House of God (Kabaah) from the filth of idolatry.
  - Take Kabaah from the possession of the polytheists and punish them.
- God informed the Muslims that this would not be an easy task, and there would be many obstacles on the way – they would be tested with the loss of property and life as a result.
- However, they were promised that if they remained patient and steadfast, ultimately, they would be the winners.

وَ لَنَبْلُوَنَّكُمْ بِشَىْءٍ مِّنَ الْخَوْفِ وَ الْجُوْعِ وَ نَقْصٍ مِّنَ الْاَمْوَالِ وَ الْاَنْفُسِ وَ الثَّمَرٰتِ ؕ وَ بَشِّرِ الصّٰبِرِيْنَ

And We will most certainly test you with something of fear and hunger and loss of property and lives and fruits, but give good news to the people who remain patient (Baqarah:155)

The Opening of Makkah

Preparation to Attack Makkah

- After the cancellation of the Treaty and all agreements (which were not time-bound), the Prophet began to prepare for a final blow to the Quraysh.

- He sent ambassadors to all the allied tribes that had recently accepted Islam to motivate them and prepare for the mission to open Makkah to Islam. They were told that if they believed in God and the Day of Judgment, they must reach Medina during Ramadan for this mission.

- The importance of this task is evident in that the Prophet had never asked for help from the allied tribes before.

اَلَا تُقَاتِلُوْنَ قَوْمًا نَّكَثُوْا اَيْمَانَهُمْ وَ هَمُّوْا بِاِخْرَاجِ الرَّسُوْلِ وَ هُمْ بَدَءُوْكُمْ اَوَّلَ مَرَّةٍ ۚ اَتَخْشَوْنَهُمْ ۚ فَاللّٰهُ اَحَقُّ اَنْ تَخْشَوْهُ اِنْ كُنْتُمْ مُّؤْمِنِيْنَ

(O believers), Will you still not fight the people who have violated their oaths, plotted to expel the Messenger, and started this war with you? Are you afraid of them? Then know that God is much more worthy than you fear Him, if you are true believers. (Surah Tawbah: 13)

- The message from the verse: God cannot allow a group of people who are on the wrong side to continue to violate the rights of the people who are on the right side, and that is a good motivation for believers to act.

- It is said that close to 10000 people joined in this journey toward Makkah.

- Historians have differed on whether the Prophet kept this mission secret or whether it was known to everyone, including Quraysh. However, it is hard to believe that a mission involving more than 10,000 people could be kept secret even in those times.

Incident of Hatib bin Baltaah

- A companion named Hatib bin Baltaah sent a letter from Medina to Makkah to some of his friends, informing them about the attack of the Muslims – a woman took the letter to Makkah.

- His family was still in Makkah (kind of hostage), and there was no one there to support them. He was afraid that Quraysh might react and harm his family in retaliation.

- The letter suggested that the Prophet was coming with a large army that would cover Quraysh like a night and wash them away like a flood.
- The woman was apprehended on the way as God informed the Prophet about this letter – when Hatib was questioned, he told the real reason for the letter, and the Prophet forgave him.
- It is believed that Quraysh was aware of the preparation of the Muslims coming towards Makkah, but this letter gave them more details and the nature of the attack.

Request for Amnesty from the Quraysh

- An army of more than 10000 Muslims encamped over a large area outside Makkah.
- The Quraysh formed a delegation of three people. Abu Sufyan came out with two other men to assess the situation and meet with the Prophet.
- Abu Sufyan was the chief of the Quraysh and sought general amnesty for his people from the Prophet.
- Abu Sufyan was a very realistic person and, at the same time, the most sensible among all the remaining leaders of the Quraysh – remember, he told the truth about the Prophet in the court of Heraclius.
- He had also realized the fact that no one on earth could now stop Prophet Muhammad and his followers from taking over the Arabian Peninsula.
- His efforts to seek amnesty were a clear sign of accepting the defeat, at least politically – at the same time, he had also started pondering if he was on the right side or not.
- It is said that when the Prophet spoke to them and presented the Message of Islam one more time, they all accepted Islam and agreed to return and also convince their people.

Abu Sufyan Accepted Islam

- Prophet Muhammad asked two questions of Abu Sufyan:

"O Abu Sufyan, has the time not come when you would accept that there is no god but God?"

"Has the time not come for you to accept that I am the Messenger of God?

- Historians report multiple versions of his response. According to the most authentic one, he responded before accepting Islam:

"I had sought help from my gods in this struggle, and you had done the same from your God. Not once did we fight each other, and you were not dominant over us. If my gods had been truthful and your God had been false, I would have overcome you. Therefore, I witness that there is no god but God, and Mohammed is the messenger of God."

- Many people, including some of the leaders of the Quraysh and idolaters, saw the truth of Islam and realized that it was from God. Still, they could not find the courage to go against their tribes and traditions until they saw an opportunity to break those shackles of tribal bonding.
- That's why it is important for us that no tribal/race/group bond must stop us from accepting the truth. The sooner the better.

Entering Makkah

- After meeting the delegation, Prophet Muhammad ordered the Muslim army to march toward Makkah.

- Saad bin Ubadah, one of the leaders of Ansar, said to Abu Sufyan: "This is the day of an intense battle; the sanctity of the Kabaah will not remain. Today, God shall crush the Quraysh."

- Abu Sufyan became worried and told the Prophet. The Prophet reassured him, "This is the day of kindness; today, the sanctity of the Kabaah shall be restored. Today, God shall honor the Quraysh."
- The delegation of Quraysh was asked to enter first and announce the general amnesty for the people of Makkah if they did not fight. They are advised to remain indoors.
- The Prophet ordered the army to stop just outside the city center, at a place in the suburb called *Dhu Tuwa*.

Torah predicted this event thousands of years ago

"The LORD came from Mount Sinai and dawned upon us from Mount Seir; <u>he shone forth from Mount Faran (Arabia) with 10,000 holy ones. He held a flaming Law in his right hand.</u>" (Bible 33:2)

Strict Instructions given to the Muslim Army

- Not to kill anyone or to be the first to use weapons – you can only defend yourself.
- The entry into Makkah must be completely peaceful.
- Khalid bin Walid to enter from the South, and Zubair bin Al Awwam from the North.
- Respect the delegation of Quraysh, especially that of Abu Sufyan, and if someone comes under his protection, they must be protected.

- Some young men from the Quraysh tried to stop Khalid bin Walid and created a riot-like situation, but the resistance was very weak, and all of them were killed.
- When the Prophet heard about these killings, he got agitated. He was informed that it was not due to the Muslims, and it happened in self-defense.
- Other than the entry into Makkah, it was peaceful.

First Thing First

- He performed circumambulation around Kabaah.
- He kissed the black stone.
- He shouted Allah O Akbar, and everyone behind him.
- He prayed two Rakah and drank Zam Zam water.
- He called Uthman bin Talha, who kept the keys to the Kabaah, and took them, opening the door.

- He then performed two Rakah inside Kabaah.

- He threw all the idols to the ground and wiped out all the pictures and sketches of them.
- He cleaned and washed the Kabaah thoroughly while reciting verse 81 of Surah Isra (on the right).
- The Prophet returned the keys to Uthman bin Talha, saying, "This is the day of loyalty. Keep this with you always. Except for the evildoers, no one shall be able to steal it from you."

وَ قُلْ جَآءَ الْحَقُّ وَ زَهَقَ الْبَاطِلُ ۚ اِنَّ الْبَاطِلَ كَانَ زَهُوْقًا

Truth has arrived, and falsehood has perished; indeed, falsehood is bound to perish (Isra: 81)

After the victory

Address in the Haram

- He asked people to gather around the Kabaah, and he stood at the door of the Kabaah and addressed the people:
  - He declared that Tawhid (the oneness of God) and the worship of God alone are the core of Islam.
  - He declared that God has no partners and no associates.
  - Except for the service of protecting the Kabaah and providing water and food to the pilgrims, all the political and social responsibilities that Quraysh had previously borne were seized by the Muslim ruler from Medina.
  - He told Quraysh that Islam does not consider any special status based on family or tribal association and that all humans are equal and the children of the same father, Adam. God judges people based on their piety.
  - He said: "There is no god but God; no one is associated with Him. He has fulfilled His promise, helped His servant, and defeated all His enemies single-handedly."

لا إلهَ إلا اللهُ وَحْدَه ، صَدَقَ وعْدَه ، ونَصَر عَبْدَه ،

وأَعَزَّ جُنْدَهُ وهَزَمَ الأَحْزابَ وحْدَه

> **Note:** We recite these sentences as part of the Takbeerat on Eid.

The Prophet of Mercy

- He asked the people of Makkah: "What kind of treatment do you expect from me?"
- They said: "Brotherly treatment. You are a kind brother and the son of a kind brother."
- The Prophet said: "I say to you what my brother Prophet Yusuf had said to his brothers: "There is no accusation upon you today", go! You are all free".
- The last words of the Prophet did not imply that he had somehow captured them. What he means by that is that he is forgiving everyone despite all the wrongs committed towards him and his fellow Muslims, and he is not going to take any revenge for the oppression of the Quraysh.
- Many people in Makkah accepted Islam simply by observing the Prophet's beautiful gesture.
- Some people asked for time to think and ponder the Quran and this situation, and later accepted Islam.

> وَمَا أَرْسَلْنَاكَ إِلَّا رَحْمَةً لِلْعَالَمِينَ
>
> And We have not sent you, [O Muhammad], except as a mercy to the worlds. (Surah Anbiya: 107)

Purifying the Haram

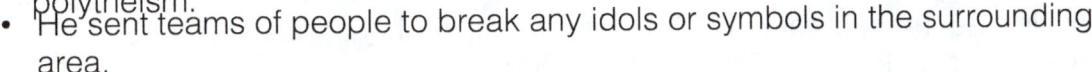

- The Prophet returned Haram to its original state, as it was built by the Prophets Ibrahim and Ismail and given to the true inheritors of their faith.
- The Prophet sent different missions to the nearby tribes to invite them to Islam and asked people to eliminate any signs or symbols of polytheism.
- He sent teams of people to break any idols or symbols in the surrounding area.
- He sent Khalid bin Walid to bring down the Uzza idol. When he came back, the Prophet said, "Now, no one shall worship Uzza."
- He sent an Ansari to break the statue of Manat, whom the tribes of Khazraj used to worship.
- The goal was to cleanse the Qiblah of Muslims from any sign of Shirk.
- He laid out the boundaries of the Haram so people would be careful and no one would worship anyone or anything other than the one true God, especially in this area.

Some Important Decisions

- The migrants were under the impression that, upon their return to Makkah, their homeland properties would be handed over to them. The Prophet told them that they had made Hijrah for the sake of God and that they would be rewarded with much better homes in the Hereafter.

- The Ansars were concerned that, after the opening of Makkah, the Prophet would remain there, but he reassured them that he would live and die in Medina.

- He made it clear to the people that "there is no migration after the opening of Makkah," – meaning the migration is not meant to move from one place to another; it is for the sake of Allah, and the reward of migration was only for the people who did it at the time of difficulty and challenge.

- He also instructed people to follow the Shariah (Law) as given by God.

Fatimah, from a noble family, was brought to the Prophet due to her habit of stealing other people's wealth. She was brought as a culprit in the court of the Prophet. Her relatives pleaded with the Prophet, but he said, "Previous nations got destroyed because of such an attitude when they had different laws for the poor and the rich. By God, if my daughter Fatimah had committed such a crime, I would have punished her."

Opening of Makkah changed everything

- One of the biggest benefits of the opening of Makkah was that many tribes and leaders from Makkah and the surrounding areas who had not fought the Prophet accepted Islam without a struggle.

- They were waiting for this event to occur before they made this decision. The entire Arabian Peninsula accepted Islam without a single fight because they followed the people of Makkah in matters of religion.

- When the people of Makkah accepted Islam, they did so with the certainty that only a Prophet of God could bring such a significant change. This was God's sole reason for selecting a Prophet from Quraysh.

- God described this amazing situation in the Quran in this small Surah:

إِذَا جَآءَ نَصْرُ اللّٰهِ وَ الْفَتْحُ ۙ وَ رَأَيْتَ النَّاسَ يَدْخُلُوْنَ فِیْ دِیْنِ اللّٰهِ اَفْوَاجًا

فَسَبِّحْ بِحَمْدِ رَبِّکَ وَ اسْتَغْفِرْهُ ؕ اِنَّهٗ کَانَ تَوَّابًا

When Allah's help comes, the victory is achieved. And you see people entering the religion of Allah in huge numbers. Then raise the praises of your Lord and ask forgiveness of Him. Indeed, He is ever accepting of repentance (Surah Nasr: 1-3)

The Owner of all Sovereignty / The Owner of All Dominions

- God is the one who owns every single thing in this Universe – whatever is in the Heavens and the Earth.
- He is the King or the Ruler of the entire Universe – many people are the kings of their countries only.
- God grants authority or rulership to human beings in this world, whoever He wishes, but the ultimate Rulership is with Him alone.
- This is God who makes some nations powerful enough to rule the world, and they become superpowers – E.g., we know that the first African countries ruled the world, then Arabs, and now the Europeans.

قُلِ اللّٰهُمَّ مٰلِكَ الْمُلْكِ تُؤْتِى الْمُلْكَ مَنْ تَشَآءُ وَ تَنْزِعُ الْمُلْكَ مِمَّنْ تَشَآءُ وَ تُعِزُّ مَنْ تَشَآءُ وَ تُذِلُّ مَنْ تَشَآءُ ۚ بِيَدِكَ الْخَيْرُ ۚ اِنَّكَ عَلٰى كُلِّ شَىْءٍ قَدِيْرٌ

Say, O Prophet, "O Allah! The Owner of all the Dominions! You give kingship to whoever You want and take it away from whoever You want; You honor whoever You want and disgrace whoever You want —all good is in Your Hands. Surely, You alone are in control of everything. (Surah Aal-e-Imran: 26)

SEERAH ACTIVITY

THE STORY OF PROPHET YUSUF

Review the story of Prophet Yusuf (AS) from Surah Yusuf and complete the True (T) and False (F) below.

T/F

1. Prophet Yusuf was from the Children of Israel ....
2. Prophet Yusuf had eight brothers ....
3. His brothers loved him so much ....
4. Allah gifted him to interpret dreams ....
5. He was the son of Prophet Shoaib ....
6. He was thrown into a well by his brothers ....
7. He was raised in a palace in Egypt............
8. He was thrown into prison because of a big........ mistake he committed
9. The King made him in charge of the treasury.......... and food
10. He was very unkind to his brothers when they......... came to get the food
11. He forgave his brothers when they were.................. helpless
12. Surah Yusuf describes the full story of Prophet......... Yusuf

Chapter 17

Some incidents after the Opening of Makkah

In this chapter, we will cover a few incidents that occurred immediately after Makkah's victory and tested the believers once more.

After the Victory

- Let's look at some of the events that occurred immediately after the opening of Makkah and tested the true believers on more time.

1. The Battle with Hawazin or Hunayn

- Despite seeing the victory of Muslims in Makkah, the tribes of Hawazin and Thaqif, living close to Taif, decided to fight the Muslims.
- Their intentions were:
  - They want to protect paganism or idol worship. They realized that with Makkah conquered, there was no stopping monotheism from spreading.
  - The Quraysh have been vanquished, so they wanted to become the new custodians of the *Kabaah*.
- Around 12,000 Muslims left for a place named Awtas, where, according to the informers, Hawazin and allies gathered almost 20,000 people to fight the Muslims.
- There were 10000 Muslims from Medina and 2000 Muslims from Makkah.
- Some new Muslims showed pride when leaving for Awtas, thinking that now no one could stand their ground in front of them – they were talking about a short-lived battle that would be over within hours.
- The reason was that the Muslims had so much weaponry and artillery, and they had never had so many horses and camels. One of them even said, "How can we possibly be destroyed when we are 12,000?"
- Prophet Muhammad did not approve of this attitude and warned them that God does not approve of boasting in His cause.
- Hawazin were famous for their archery skills, and they posted archers atop hills and in narrow valleys to surprise the Muslims.
- They attacked them as soon as they saw the first row of Muslims, and it caused panic among Muslims, causing them to scatter.
- The Prophet realized the situation, gathered his close companions and Ansars, and launched a concentrated attack on Hawazin.
- At this stage, he threw sand toward the enemy and prayed to God for victory.
- The Hawazin could not keep their feet on the ground after that and began running in different directions.
- The Prophet and Muslims surrounded the city of Taif and laid a siege for 18 days until the disbelievers gave up.

2. A large amount of war treasure in hand

- Hawazin left everything in this chaos, and a large amount of war treasure came into the hands of Muslims.
- After keeping 1/5th for God and His Messenger (as per the law of the Quran), he distributed most of the wealth, including livestock, among the leaders of the tribes who had recently accepted Islam.
- It was a message to them that the Prophet and the Muslims do not fight for wealth but for the sake of God.
- These leaders were impressed by the Prophet's generosity.
- Some people from Hawazin came and repented for their mistakes in front of the Prophet and accepted Islam – they requested the Prophet to return their prisoners and property, as the war had put them under difficult financial conditions.
- The Prophet freed their prisoners and returned his portion, as well as the portion of Banu Abdul Muttalib (his family). He also appealed to others to return whatever property they could.
- The Prophet's appeal and his act of kindness affected the entire army, and all of them returned their portion to Hawazin.

Complaints by the Ansar

- Some young men of Ansar were not happy with this distribution, and they considered it a display of favoritism towards the tribes of the Quraysh, to which the Prophet belonged.
- When the Prophet heard that, first he explained why he did that, and then he had a dialogue with the Ansar:

"O' Ansar! When I had come to you, were you not misguided? Then God guided you. Were you not deprived? Then God gave you wealth. Were you not each other's enemies? Then God placed love in your hearts." They admitted, "God and His Messenger were their greatest supporters." "O' Ansar! Are you not satisfied that other people may return with livestock and some wealth while you take the Messenger of God to your homes? By God! What you take with you is much better than what others take with them." (meaning their reward will be Jannah) At this, the Ansar said with one voice: "O' Messenger of God! We are happy with your decision."

Worldly Benefits

OR

Paradise in the Hereafter

Powerful Compeller

- God is the Compeller, the Irresistible, because He is mighty, and nothing can come in His way to stop Him.
- He is in absolute control of everything, and no one can resist Him if He wants to achieve something.
- To get an idea of His Powers, we should look around the universe.
- This is one of those names that are intense and only befitting of God. It does not fit as a quality of a human being (no one likes to compel or force someone).
- God is Extremely Powerful, but at the same time, He is Wise and Merciful, meaning He uses His Powers very wisely and only where they are needed.
- Armies of people, regardless of power and weapons, cannot withstand His power if He decides to defeat them.

هُوَ اللّٰهُ الَّذِىْ لَآ اِلٰهَ اِلَّا هُوَ ۚ اَلْمَلِكُ الْقُدُّوْسُ السَّلٰمُ الْمُؤْمِنُ الْمُهَيْمِنُ الْعَزِيْزُ
الْجَبَّارُ الْمُتَكَبِّرُ ۚ سُبْحٰنَ اللّٰهِ عَمَّا يُشْرِكُوْنَ

He is the very God besides whom there is no deity, the Sovereign Lord, the Holy, the Embodiment of Peace, the Giver of Tranquility, the Guardian, the Mighty, the Powerful Compeller, the Most High; exalted is God above what they state as partners!

Chapter 18

Expedition of Tabuk

In this chapter, we will cover the expedition to Tabuk that became a test for many hypocrites and Muslims.

The Expedition of Tabuk

The Background

- The tribes and the Arabs living in northern Arabia were very loyal to the Roman Empire and the king because of their influence.

- The powerful Roman government was not disregarding the victories of Islam in Arabia, especially under Heraclius, who realized early on that no one could stop the Prophet and Islam from taking over this empire.

- He could not find the courage to accept Islam when he received the letter from the Prophet.

- Worried about his rulership, he partnered with many Arabian tribes to stop the Muslims from reaching North – he thought attacking Medina would be a better option than sitting in the north.

- The Prophet was informed and decided to deal with this force in the North, but the border was far away, and the weather was very hot – he needed special preparation.

- He appealed to all the Muslims to donate whatever they could and help in this expedition, as it was against one of the largest empires in that area.

The Preparation and Generosity of Muslims

- The sincere Muslims answered the appeal and contributed more than they could afford.

- The companion Omar wanted to excel and beat Abu Bakr in this 'competition,' so he contributed half of his wealth. Abu Bakr brought everything he had in his house, and when the Prophet asked, "Did you leave anything at home?" he replied, "Yes, God and His Messenger." The companion Uthman sponsored one-third of the entire army.

- Women handed over their jewelry to prepare for the war; even the poorest gave something.

- Some men, who did not have their animals to ride, approached the Prophet requesting him for the ride so they could also participate – the Prophet excused them, and they returned feeling dejected and sad.

- A general announcement was made, "Come out, whether you are light or heavy" – meaning, regardless of whether you are rich or poor.

- This expedition became a huge test for some people as it was high summer, and the harvest was ready. Plus, the journey was difficult due to the distance and extreme heat.

A Test of Faith and Loyalty

- Like other similar occasions, this expedition became a test for the weaker Muslims and the hypocrites.
- Some said it was too hot and Muslims would die on their way.
- Some said that the Roman army was not an easy target, and Muslims would perish.

The Test of Faith

- Abdullah bin Ubayy, the chief hypocrite, tried to weaken the morale by saying, "It is no game to go in this heat and fight one of the strongest armies in the world."
- They began mocking people who showed great valor and generosity.
- Affected by this, many good Muslims also came to the Prophet and presented their excuses – religious reasons (they don't have that strong faith), family, business, harvest etc.
- Some very sincere Muslims did not join at first, thinking they would finish their affairs at home first and then join the army – but that never happened, as they got busy with other daily life issues.
- Three early Muslim companions were among them: Kaab bin Malik, Hilal bin Umayyah, and Murrah bin Rabi.
- It is also reported that the People of the Book were behind inciting the Romans to wage this war - they maintained communication with the hypocrites of Medina.
- God continued to use such events in the process of removing hypocrites from the ranks of Muslims.

Why does fighting for God's sake become a huge test for people at the time of the Prophets?

The Mosque of 'Harm'

- The Jews wanted to influence the hypocrites and the Muslim affairs in Medina, and for that, they asked the hypocrites to build a mosque in the suburbs of Medina.

- The motives behind building this mosque were:
  - Give hypocrites a place of their own to gather and conspire.
  - To launch campaigns against Muslims in the guise of Islam.
  - Created differences among Muslims.

- The hypocrites requested the Prophet to inaugurate it by leading the first prayer – the inauguration got postponed due to the preparation for Tabuk.

- It was surprising that the same people who built this mosque refused to give anything for the expedition when asked.

- God revealed the verses in the Quran forbidding the Prophet to even stand in that mosque – God exposed the plan and called that mosque "a mosque for causing harm, disbelief, and division among the believers".

What Happened in Tabuk

- The Prophet arrived in Tabuk with a force of 30,000 soldiers and 10,000 horses.

- The Romans got discouraged seeing the size of the army and did not confront the Muslims.

- The Prophet stayed in Tabuk for three weeks. After that, he announced the return.

- While the Prophet and his army were in Tabuk, they took care of some of the smaller states that were controlling the routes to Syria and Iraq.

- Many rulers in the region became afraid of Muslims and preferred to develop peaceful relations with them, deciding to stop supporting Roman rulers.

- The mission of Tabuk had instilled awe among Muslims in the northern Arab states and regions under its influence.

Dealing with the hypocrites

- God revealed verses that instructed the Prophet to stop adopting a softer attitude towards the hypocrites.
- The Prophet announced among the Muslims that, until permission is given, no one will talk to the hypocrites or have any social interactions with them.
- As the head of the state, the Prophet also ordered the demolition of the mosque that the hypocrites built to divide the Muslims and conspire (make plans) against the state.
- The hypocrites were informed that this behavior would be remembered and that they would be dealt with at the right time.
- Many sincere Muslims who were lazy in carrying out the instructions at the time of preparing for the mission showed regret and asked God and His Messenger for forgiveness, and they were pardoned (forgiven).

The Affair of Three Sincere Muslims

- God gave special instructions to the three sincere Muslims who decided not to go with the Prophet.
- Especially, Kaab bin Malik told the entire story in a hadith that, although he was well-off and had the means to go, the worldly benefits kept him away.
- They all admitted their mistakes and were ready to do whatever it took to make amends.

- God asked the Prophet and the Muslims to boycott them socially, and even their wives left them temporarily.
- They were ready to give up all their wealth and donate it for the sake of God, hoping to see His and His Messenger's forgiveness – the Prophet had to wait for God's decision.
- Finally, God revealed verses in the Quran about their forgiveness.
- The Prophet's companions went through severe tests and trials in their lives. They were tested by losing their homeland, homes, property, wealth, livelihoods, lives, relationships, etc.
- The reason for such a severe test was that God promised them Paradise in the Hereafter while they were still alive. Since the Messenger of God was among them and had a mission to complete, they had no choice but to leave him in the middle of it until it was finished. They sacrificed so much for that, and that's why Paradise was their reward.

The Possessor of Pride and Greatness

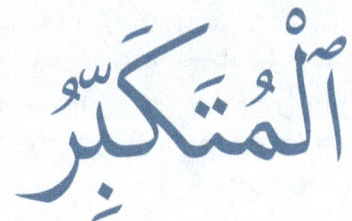

- God calls Himself the Possessor of Pride and Greatness – He is Supremely Great.

- God teaches human beings not to be arrogant, and this is one of those names that should make people humble. Human beings are weak, and if they understand the Supreme Greatness of God, they will never be arrogant.

- This is also one of those names that are intense and only befitting of God. It does not suit as one of the qualities of a human being.

- On the contrary, the greatness of human beings is in their humbleness and humility toward God and also toward other fellow beings.

هُوَ اللّٰهُ الَّذِىْ لَآ اِلٰهَ اِلَّا هُوَ ۚ اَلْمَلِكُ الْقُدُّوْسُ السَّلٰمُ الْمُؤْمِنُ الْمُهَيْمِنُ الْعَزِيْزُ الْجَبَّارُ الْمُتَكَبِّرُ ۚ سُبْحٰنَ اللّٰهِ عَمَّا يُشْرِكُوْنَ

He is the very God besides whom there is no deity, the Sovereign Lord, the Holy, the Embodiment of Peace, the Giver of Tranquility, the Guardian, the Mighty, the Powerful Compeller, the Most High; exalted is God above what they state as partners!

SEERAH ACTIVITY

STORYTELLING

Read the story of the companion <u>Kaab Ibn Malik</u> (RA) and narrate his story in your own words in 2-3 minutes.

Instructions

- Read or hear the story from the following sources, or what you already have:

  https://yaqeeninstitute.org/watch/series/kaab-ibn-malik-ra-the-greatest-story-of-repentance-the-firsts

  https://www.youtube.com/watch?v=GlBudCxr63o

- Summarize the story in 2-3 minutes as the narrator recounts it.

- You can add your comments and details if you'd like.

- In the end, convey the moral or lesson learned from the story to everyone.

Chapter 19

Final Warning

In this chapter, we will cover the Final Warning the Messengers give to their nations before the final punishment was announced and carried out. This is one of God's practices.

The Final Warning

The Announcement of Final Warning

- Allah did not want to punish anyone who had the slightest inclination to accept the truth when the Messenger was among them.
- Right after the victory of Makkah, the idolaters performed Hajj as they used to before, because the Prophet and his companions were busy dealing with the Christian nations in the North.

- In the 9th AH, the Prophet sent 300 companions to Makkah under the leadership of Abu Bakr to bring the Hajj rites (procedures) back to their original form.
- Right after them, he sent Ali as his special messenger to Makkah to announce the verses of Surah Tawbah, in which God gave a final warning to the Idolators.
- The occasion of Hajj was used so that everyone from almost every tribe would hear the warning.

The Announcement

- From now on, no idolator will be allowed to perform Umrah or Hajj. They will not be allowed to circumambulate (tawaf) the Kabaah nude (they invented this practice to get close to their idols).
- Idolaters will be prohibited from entering the Haram.

- The Hajj and Umrah will be performed only as per the Sunnah of the Prophet Ibrahim.
- All agreements are considered canceled.
- Idolators have four months from that day to make up their mind, and they have the following choices:
  - Accept Islam, pray, and pay Zakah OR.
  - Surrender themselves to the Islamic government, and they will be either executed for the crime of rejecting a Messenger or expelled from this land.
- The People of the Book were given the following choices: Accept Islam, pay Jizyah (a tax), accept the authority of Muslims, or be ready to fight.
- The final warnings appeared in Surah Taubah, and this is the only Surah that does not start with **Bismillah** because it is a Surah of punishment.

بَرَآءَةٌ مِّنَ اللّٰهِ وَ رَسُوْلِهٖۤ اِلَى الَّذِيْنَ عَاهَدْتُّمْ مِّنَ الْمُشْرِكِيْنَ

فَسِيْحُوْا فِى الْاَرْضِ اَرْبَعَةَ اَشْهُرٍ وَّ اعْلَمُوْۤا اَنَّكُمْ غَيْرُ مُعْجِزِى اللّٰهِ ۙ وَ اَنَّ اللّٰهَ مُخْزِى الْكٰفِرِيْنَ

وَ اَذَانٌ مِّنَ اللّٰهِ وَ رَسُوْلِهٖۤ اِلَى النَّاسِ يَوْمَ الْحَجِّ الْاَكْبَرِ اَنَّ اللّٰهَ بَرِىْٓءٌ مِّنَ الْمُشْرِكِيْنَ ۙ وَ رَسُوْلُهٗ ؕ فَاِنْ

تُبْتُمْ فَهُوَ خَيْرٌ لَّكُمْ ۚ وَ اِنْ تَوَلَّيْتُمْ فَاعْلَمُوْۤا اَنَّكُمْ غَيْرُ مُعْجِزِى اللّٰهِ ؕ وَ بَشِّرِ الَّذِيْنَ كَفَرُوْا بِعَذَابٍ اَلِيْمٍ

[This is a declaration of] dissociation, from Allah and His Messenger, to those with whom you had made a treaty among the polytheists. So, (tell them) to travel freely through the land for the next four months, but know that you cannot overpower Allah and that Allah will (finally) disgrace the disbelievers. And [it is] an announcement from Allah and His Messenger to the people on the day of the greater pilgrimage that Allah is disassociated from the disbelievers, and [so is] His Messenger. So, if you repent, that is best for you; but if you turn away - then know that you will not cause failure to Allah. And give the news to those who disbelieve of a painful punishment. (Surah Tawbah:1-4)

The Year of Delegations

1. Right after the Battle of the Trench, many tribal groups started to meet the Prophet; some accepted Islam, and others learned about it.

2. After the victory of Makkah, no tribe in Arabia was in any doubt about Islam being the only power in the whole region and about the punishment that they may face from God, like Quraysh.

3. In the 9th AH, many delegations met the Prophet, and that's why it is called the Year of Delegations (groups).

4. Many of them accepted Islam, but some of them just wanted to make a peace treaty and agreed to accept Muslim authority in the region.

5. The historians agreed that more than 250-300 delegations came to Medinah in that year.

6. Some of the famous tribes that came were:
Banu Thaqif from Taif
Banu Saad (to which the foster mother of the Prophet belongs)
Banu Harith from Yemen
Abd Al Qays from Bahrain
Banu Muharib
Banu Kalb
Banu Daws (the tribe of Abu Huraira)
Banu Hanifa
Tribe of Himyar

The Delegation from Najran

- Najran was the largest Christian center near the border of Yemen and maintained a strong relationship with the Roman Empire.
- Many leading members and bishops came to Medina and met the Prophet.
- They stayed in Medina and asked many questions about Islam.

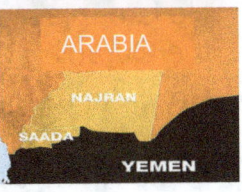

- The Prophet read to them verses from the Quran about Prophet Jesus and told them of his actual position in the sight of God (a great Prophet).

- It sounds strange that the delegation of Christians recognized Prophet Muhammad as the true Prophet of God, but did not accept Islam. It is said that out of 60 people who visited, 24 were from the society's elite, and a few were senior bishops. When discussing the matter of the Prophet among themselves, one of the bishop brothers asked, "Why didn't we accept him if he is the true Prophet of God?" The bishop replied, "Do you wish to give up all of the wealth and privileges that the (Roman) emperor has given us?" When the younger brother heard this, he was so shocked. He went back to Medina and accepted Islam.

- The Quran gave a very strange instruction to the Prophet – he was told that both Prophet Muhammad and their leaders would say the following:
- "The curse of God be upon the ones among us who are the liars."
- They knew in their hearts that they were expecting a Prophet, and Prophet Muhammad was that Messenger, so they got afraid and agreed to pay Jizyah (tax) to the Muslims.
- During their stay, whenever they had their prayer times, the Prophet allowed them to pray in the mosque.
- When the delegation returned to Najran and the Archbishop learned the details from them, he said, "Indeed, this man is a Prophet and Messenger of God."

Musaylimah Al Kadhdhab (false prophet)

- Prophet Muhammad said: "After my death, you shall see 30 false prophets that are liars." The first was Musaylimah." (Hadith)

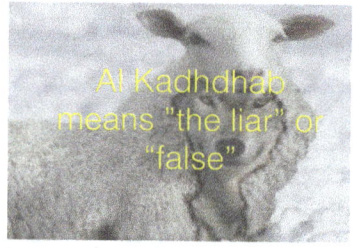

Al Kadhdhab means "the liar" or "false"

- Musaylimah was a Christian leader of the Banu Hanifa tribe and, due to his knowledge of languages and scriptures, earned considerable respect among his tribesmen.
- When his delegation came to meet the Prophet, he proposed the following: "If the Prophet gives me power after his death, then I'll follow him. And he must share with me in prophethood as Musa AS shared with his brother Harun AS."
- The Prophet told him that the Messengers and the Prophet do not come to gain worldly benefits, and that they leave no wealth behind.
- He later claimed prophethood and used to recite made-up verses, like those in the Quran.
- He wrote a letter to the Prophet, saying, "From Musaylimah, the messenger of God, to Muhammad, the Messenger of God. I have been given a share in this matter with you. Half the earth belongs to us and a half to the Quraysh, but Quraysh are people who sin."
- After the death of the Prophet, when Abu Bakr had to fight a war with a tribe that had threatened the Muslims, Musaylimah was killed by the Muslims.

The Guide　　True  اَلْهَادِي

- If anyone is looking for guidance on the right path, he/she should ask Allah, because the Quran says, "Guidance comes only from Him."
- Allah's guidance is entirely dependent on how much effort we have put in – it does not come automatically.
- When we want to tell someone about something right then, our job is to deliver the message – we should not force people to accept something.
- That is the reason we pray to Allah in every Salah, reciting Surah Fatiha, in which we ask for guidance.
- A good example is the group of Christians who came from Najran and learned that Prophet Muhammad is the true Prophet of God, but they still did not accept Islam due to the meager worldly benefits. Since they did not intend to accept the Truth, Allah did not guide them.

اِهْدِ نَا الصِّرَاطَ الْمُسْتَقِيْمَ

(O God), guide us to the straight path (Surah Fatiha:5).

ARABIC CALLIGRAPHY COMPETITION

Pick one name of Allah other than Allah and create a Colored Calligraphy Artwork by hand (Example below)

- Al-Nasir – The Helper
- Allah O Akbar – Allah is the Greatest
- Al-Shakoor – Most Grateful
- Al-Momin – the Source of Security & Peace
- Al-Ghafoor – the Most Forgiving
- Al-Wakeel – The Disposer of Affairs
- Al-Qawee – The All-Strong
- Al-Musawwir – The Designer
- Al-Malik – The King

Instructions

- Be creative and try to create your own art without copying from the internet.

- Pick an attribute/name of Allah from above that you love the most.

- The artwork should not be smaller than a standard paper size (11 x 8).

- You can add a theme, graphics, or a picture related to the attributes of Allah.

Chapter 20

The Farewell Sermon

In this chapter, we will cover the Hajj that the Prophet Muhammad performed and the Final Sermon he delivered, which summarizes the core values of Islam in the most beautiful way.

The only Hajj and the Final Sermon to Muslims

- Before we talk about one of the most significant events in the life of the Prophet Muhammad, let's talk about the compilation of the Quran in the lifetime of the Prophet Muhammad.
- Many historians claim that the Quran was not compiled during the time of the Prophet Muhammad and that it was compiled later by Caliph Abu Bakr.

The Compilation of the Quran

- During the Ramadan of 10 AH, the Angel Gabriel and the Prophet Muhammad recited the complete Quran to each other twice in its final form. Some other companions were also present.

- The Quran was revealed in one order but compiled in another, as God instructed.

- The verses of Surah Qiyamah, Aala, and some of the other Surahs clearly indicate that God promised to collect the Quran in the lifetime of the Prophet, and before the Prophet's death, it was presented to the Prophet in its final form.
- This final recital (after the collection) is also termed Al Ardah Al Akhirah (the Final Presentation).
- Besides the Quran, many Ahadith also record the compilation and final recitation of the Quran in the lifetime of the Prophet.
- The Quran is the only book in the history of the world whose text and reading have been preserved. For example, how to recite the letters, words, and verses was also preserved.

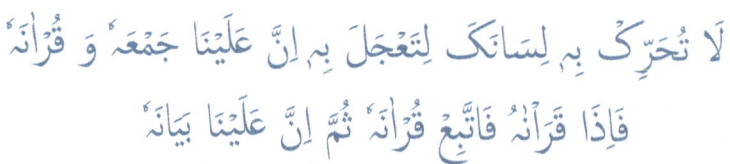

لَا تُحَرِّكْ بِهٖ لِسَانَکَ لِتَعْجَلَ بِهٖ اِنَّ عَلَيْنَا جَمْعَهٗ وَ قُرْاٰنَهٗ

فَاِذَا قَرَاْنٰهُ فَاتَّبِعْ قُرْاٰنَهٗ ثُمَّ اِنَّ عَلَيْنَا بَيَانَهٗ

O Prophet!] To quickly acquire this (Quran), do not move your tongue in haste (fast); Rest assured, upon Us is its collection and recital. So, when [at that time] We recite it, follow that recital (reading) of it. Then upon Us is to explain it [for you wherever need be]. (75:16-19)

The Farewell Hajj

- The final recital was the sign that the Prophet's mission was about to be completed.
- There was one more thing that Prophet Muhammad wanted to practically show the Muslims, as thousands of new Muslims joined this religion.

- Quraish used to perform Hajj before this time, but they introduced so many innovations to it.
- The Prophet decided to do the Hajj in 10 AH, showing them how to perform it correctly, following the Sunnah of Prophet Ibrahim.
- The Prophet used this opportunity to train Muslims on the authentic practices of Hajj that were distorted by the idolaters.
- The Prophet specifically told them, "Take your rites of Hajj from me." The Prophet performed one Hajj; therefore, all guidance regarding Hajj comes from that one Hajj.
- He left for Makkah with tens of thousands of Muslims.
- It is said that more than 100,000 performed the Hajj that year with the Prophet.
- **Remember:** Close to **100 Muslims** migrated to Medinah from Makkah just 10 years ago.

The Final Sermon

- As we said, the Prophet gave multiple khutbahs, one in Arafat and 2-3 in Mina.
- On the Day of Arafah of that year, it happened to be a Friday. And the Prophet said, "This is the day of al-Hajj al-Akbar.
- In Hajj, there is a Khutbah (speech) of Hajj that an Imam delivers. Prophet Muhammad delivered that Khutbah, which is written in history like a shining object.
- One of the final verses of the Quran, such as Surah Al-Maida, verse 3, was revealed.
- "O' People! Listen to me carefully because I don't think that I shall be able to meet you here after this year."

Today. I have completed your religion for you, and have completed my favor upon you, and have chosen Islam as your religion. (5:3)

The Final Sermon – Important Points

1 **Sanctity of human life:** It was the month of Dhul Hijjah, the day of Arafa, and the city of Makkah; all of them were blessed and sacred. He said that the life, property, and honor of every human being are as sacred as these three things, so one should not violate them.

2 **Accountability:** The people will meet their Creator soon, and He will ask them about their deeds, so be careful.

3 **Trust and Honesty:** People should honor and protect the trust others have placed in them.

4 **Usury is prohibited:** People cannot charge interest on loans they have made to others. Their right is only to the actual money loaned (in other words, you cannot charge interest on the money loaned to someone).

5 **Rights of spouses**: Husbands and wives should respect each other's rights, especially husbands, who must be kind to their wives.

6 **Rights of Slaves:** There were still slaves in society. The slave owners were asked to be gentle and good to their slaves, feed them what they ate, and clothe them with what they wore.

7 **Quran and Sunnah:** The Prophet has left us two things that, if we hold on to them, will never misguide us: the Quran and the Sunnah. The entire body of Islam is within these two things. Everything else is the explanation of these two,

8 **Equality:** All human beings are the children of Adam and are equal in the sight of God. The most honorable in the sight of God is the one who is the most conscious of God.

9 **No Place for Racism:** No Arab has any preference over a non-Arab, and no non-Arab has preference over an Arab. No white has a superiority over a black, and no black has a superiority over a white.

10 **Brotherhood:** All Muslims are brothers to one another. They should not take away each other's rights.

11 **Fighting Wars:** People should not go back to the old days of ignorance and start killing each other.

12 **Inheritance:** People should be careful about distributing inheritance and should not take away other people's rights in inheritance.

13 **Last Prophet:** There is no Prophet after Prophet Muhammad, and people should take care of their prayers, Zakah, Fasting, and Hajj.

14 **Society:** People should obey their elected rulers, no matter how bad they are.

Lessons from Final Sermon

- Most people associate Islam with some rituals and practices. But when you look at the final sermon of Prophet Muhammad, it's all about:
  - How do we act as human beings in front of God
  - How do we treat our fellow beings, and how to perfect our morals for that
- People typically refer to the United Nations (UN) Charter of Human Rights when discussing human rights. This was adopted by most countries worldwide in 1948. However, the Final Sermon of the Prophet shows that he gave this charter to humanity 1500 years ago.
- There is much to learn from the Prophet's last sermon, not only for Muslims but also for the global community.
- However, it will not be effective if we, as Muslims, do not abide by these principles outlined by the Prophet. We should practice what we preach.
- Once we practice it, only then will we be in a position to take this message to the rest of humanity.

The Prophet Delivered the Message – We Got it

In the end, he said:
"O' my Lord! Have I not communicated the message?

A voice came from the crowd: "Yes! O Messenger of God! You have communicated the message."

At this, the Prophet said: "O God! Be a witness to this."

Then he addressed the crowd: "When asked about me, what will you say? The people said: "We will say that you have fulfilled your obligations of communicating the message; you thought of good for the Muslims; you removed the darkness of ignorance and kept trust in such a manner that was demanded by it."

The Prophet advised those present to inform those absent.

In the end, he said: "O God! Be a witness! Be a witness! Be a witness!"

Discuss the lessons learned from the final sermon.

The believers are brothers to each other

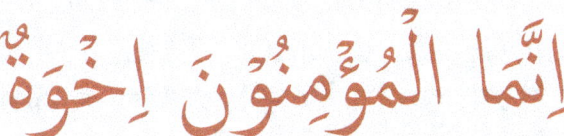

- In Arabic, these types of statements included both genders. The verse includes women automatically.
- These instructions are given in Surah Hujrat on how to deal with other Muslims.
- The Quran calls believers brothers to each other regardless of race, country, region, culture, etc.
- We should reunite brothers if they are fighting for any reason.
- We should not make fun of individuals or a group.
- We should not call them by a nickname they do not like.
- We should not spy on other people.
- We should always think positively about people, ignoring their negatives.
- We should not backbite, as it is like eating their flesh.
- Races, colors, tribes, groups, and cultures are meant to recognize and respect one another – none of these things make anyone superior.
- What makes someone superior in the sight of Allah is righteousness.

SEERAH ACTIVITY

FAREWELL SERMON WORD CLOUD

The Word Cloud is a visually engaging and meaningful way for kids to internalize the key teachings from the Farewell Sermon of Prophet Muhammad (peace be upon him)

Sample

Instructions

- Draw on poster paper (not too big) or digitally using Canva.

- Use big keywords (one or two) that represent the points mentioned in the Sermon.

- Write words in different shapes, sizes, and colors.

- Turn big ideas into something colorful, creative, and reflective.

- Prophet Muhammad (SAW) reminded Muslims of many important things, like "Equality".

- Make one word stand out that you learned or liked the most.

- Optionally, decorate with patterns, icons, and so on.

Chapter 21

The Return to God

In this chapter, we will discuss the return of the Last Prophet to God, which was the saddest moment in the lives of the Muslims.

The return to God

The Prophet Got Sick

- One night, he woke up one of his companions, Abu Muwhehi, and asked him to go with him to the graveyard of Al Baqii.

- This graveyard is next to the Mosque of the Prophet, and many famous companions and members of the Prophet's family are buried here.

- God instructed him to make dua for the people who were buried there.
- When he returned home, he started feeling headaches and ultimately developed a fever.
- He continued to perform his daily activities, but the pain and the fever continued to increase.
- He asked to move in with Aisha and stayed there while she took care of him.

The Choice to Leave the World

 VS

Jannah

- In this ill condition, he went to the mosque the next day and sat on the pulpit for many hours, and continued to pray for the martyrs of Uhud and God's mercy.
- He told his companions that God had given one of His servants (himself) the choice to remain in this world or to leave for the eternal pleasures with God alone – the servant has decided to leave.
- Abu Bakr understood that the Prophet was talking about himself, so he started to cry.
- He praised Abu Bakr and told his companions that he found no companion in this world better than Abu Bakr.
- This was an indication that he wanted Abu Bakr to lead the prayers in the mosque, and that's what he did when the Prophet's illness became severe.

Abu Bakr Led the Prayers

- When it became impossible for the Prophet to come to the Mosque and fulfill his responsibilities, he ordered Abu Bakr to lead the prayers in his place – it was a great honor for Abu Bakr.

- In the presence of Prophet Muhammad, no one can imagine that someone else will lead the Salah or lead any religious activity. But when the Prophet asked Abu Bakr to lead the prayers, it speaks volumes about the value and importance of Abu Bakr in the eyes of the Prophet Muhammad.

- Then the Prophet announced, "Let all of the doors of the Masjid that go in from the private houses be closed." But he made one exception, "Except for the door of Abu Bakr." This was an honor the Prophet bestowed on Abu Bakr.

- After the death of Prophet Muhammad, Muslims chose Abu Bakr as the next Caliph of Muslims based on his status with Prophet Muhammad.

- Aisha, the wife of the Prophet Muhammad and daughter of Abu Bakr, requested that the Prophet appoint someone else because Abu Bakr had a soft heart and would cry while reciting the Quran – the Prophet insisted that Abu Bakr lead the prayers.

Abu Bakr – The First Caliph of the Prophet of God

- After the death of the Prophet, Abu Bakr became the first Caliph, the leader of the Muslim nation.

- He was among the first few (3rd person) who accepted Islam.

- Every time he was told of something related to the Prophet, he accepted it without a single thought – for this, the Prophet gave him the nickname As-Siddiq (The Truthful).

- He ruled for around 2 years and fought wars with people who rejected Islam after the Prophet's death and refused to pay the Jizyah tax (which the non-Muslims had to pay at that time as a symbol of accepting the authority of the Prophet).

The Prophet's Advices

 "May God destroy the nation that converted the graves of its prophets into mosques." – Prophet's grave was kept outside of the mosque in his house, where he used to stay with Aisha, his wife.

 "There should not be two religions in the Arabian Peninsula." – People who do not want to accept Islam should leave this land. God has dedicated this piece of land for His worship alone.

 "If there is anyone who has any obligation or right I've not fulfilled, or any debt I haven't paid, come now and ask me before the Day of Judgement." – If people know that they are about to die, they should do their utmost to pay off their debts or fulfill any pending obligation.

 "If I have hit anybody unjustly in my whole life, then here is my back; come and hit me now before the Day of Judgement." – If we have done wrong to someone, we should ask for forgiveness before we die.

The Most Merciful

"You should have good thoughts of Allah when you are about to die." – think positively that He will treat your soul with Mercy, and He will forgive you because that's who God is.

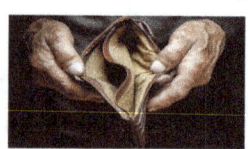 "Fear Allah with regards to the weak (poor) and oppressed of the society, the slaves and servants: Fear Allah, for they will have a chance to complain on the day of Judgement".

 "As-salah, as-salah, as-salah ……" – Be mindful of your prayers was his **LAST ADVICE.**

The departure from this world

- After the Fajr prayer of the 12th of Rabi ul Awwal, which he prayed separately in the mosque and did not lead, he went back home when the severity of his illness intensified.

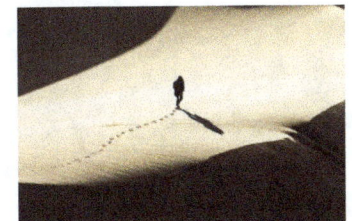

- The son of Abu Bakr visited him and brought a new Miswak (a traditional natural toothbrush used to clean teeth). Aisha noted that the Prophet was looking at it with interest, so she took it from his brother, and the Prophet cleaned his teeth properly.

No material possession

- The next morning, the day before he passed away, he asked, "How much money do I have?" Aisha found the pouches and pulled out seven silver coins. The total value is around $20 of today's dollars. This was the entire possession he had on the last day of his life.

- He held them in one hand and said, "What will I say to Allah if I meet Him with these coins?" And he handed it back to Aisha and said, "Go give it to the poor now," and he fell unconscious again.

- When he woke up, he said to Aisha, "Have you given it to the poor?" But it was not on her priority list — taking care of the Prophet came first; so she just said, "I will do it [later]." And again, he fainted, and again, he woke up saying, "Have you given it to the poor?" And he continued to ask throughout the day until Aisha realized that the Prophet would not be content until she gave away the coins.

- Thus, she got rid of everything in the house that was money.

- Our Prophet passed away without owning a single penny.

- Prophets have no desire for this world as they are happy to have all the wealth and pleasures of life in the Hereafter.

> "Be in this world as if you were a stranger or a traveler along a path."
> (Sahih Bukhari #6053)

The Seal of the Prophets

- In his last sermon, Prophet Muhammad said that no other Prophet would come after him.
- That means that Prophet Muhammad was the **"Seal of the Prophets."**
- This title means that no Prophet or Messenger will come after him, and the whole concept of prophethood has been terminated.
- God speaks to Prophets and Messengers directly, or through the Angel Gabriel, through revelation. After Prophet Muhammad, no one can claim that God is speaking to them or that they receive revelation from God.
- The purpose of Messenger and Prophets was to remind people of the Message of God, which is "There is no one worthy of worship except one True God, and one day we will be held responsible for our actions."
- That core, simple message is now permanently preserved in the Quran, and it has been with us for almost 1500 years in its original language, with absolutely no change.
- If someone wants to know the message of Islam, all they have to do is open the Quran and read the message directly from God.

مَا كَانَ مُحَمَّدٌ أَبَآ أَحَدٍ مِّن رِّجَالِكُمْ وَ لَكِن رَّسُولَ اللّٰهِ وَ خَاتَمَ النَّبِيِّنَ ۚ وَ كَانَ اللّٰهُ بِكُلِّ شَىْءٍ عَلِيمًا

[In reality,] Muhammad is the father of no male among you; in fact, he is the Messenger of God and the Seal of the Prophets. [Hence, he alone had to fulfil this responsibility], and God has knowledge of all things (Surah Ahzab:40)

GEMS FROM THE QURAN AND HADITH

OVERVIEW

Quran is the final testament of God preserved in its original language. It is the ultimate source of guidance revealed for human beings through Prophet Muhammad (PBUH) and affirms everything revealed before in the form of religious scriptures (for example, the Gospel/Bible). Being the Final Messenger of God, Prophet Muhammad (PBUH) practiced that guidance in his daily life, which is reported to us in the form of Ahadith through a chain of narrators. Building on the foundation created in Level 5, which covered various subject matters related to the Quran sciences, this course will explore various sections of the Quran, Hadith, and Bible relevant to faith and different aspects of our lives and explain those passages in a style appropriate for teenagers. This course will provide an excellent opportunity for our Muslim teenagers to build a deeper relationship with the Message of the Quran.

OBJECTIVES

◆ Apply the knowledge gained about the sciences of the Quran in Level 5 to the selected passages of the Quran.

◆ Build an understanding of the Quran by reading various sections in detail and asking questions.

◆ Understand the relationship between the Quran and Hadith and how hadith should be understood in the light of the Quran.

◆ Appreciate the fact that there is nothing wrong with reading the Bible and benefit from the wisdom that it still offers.

Ghamidi Center of Islamic Learning
An Initiative of Al-Mawrid US Inc.

ISBN 978-1-966600-30-5
90000
9 781966 600305

Lessons from his last days

- Prophet Muhammad has left with us the Quran and the Sunnah.
- We know exactly what we need to do to be successful in the hereafter. He has given us all the details, and we have no excuse to fail.
- The majority of his teachings, along with his final piece of advice, focused on our character and our relationship with God and His creation.
- The best way to build our character is to have the best company of friends around us. The best of friends are those who help you succeed in the Hereafter.
- Prophet Muhammad was not interested in collecting worldly wealth; it was not part of his nature or a personal choice. However, he never advised people to act that way because there is nothing wrong with owning wealth and taking care of their family.
- The best way to look at it is to remember that this is a temporary world and to do our best to improve our lives here, without sacrificing our hereafter.
- If we ever face the choice between the temporary benefits of this world and the lasting pleasures of the next life, we should act wisely and choose what is permanent.
- If we have done wrong to someone in this world, it's better to settle it here because on the Day of Judgment, the person you have wronged may not forgive you and take away all your good deeds.
- The final piece of advice from the Prophet is significant: Guard our salah. Salah is the only virtuous deed that, if we cling to it in our lives, will ensure we do not go astray, as it always connects us to God. Even if we make mistakes, we will always have the opportunity to turn back to God through Salah.

SEERAH ACTIVITY

POETRY/WRITING COMPETITION

Pick one topic and write a Poem or an Essay on the topic

Topics

1. The Last Sermon
2. Prophet Muhammad – A Mercy to Mankind
3. Prophet Muhammad's Final Advice(s)
4. Prophet Muhammad's Return to God
5. Brotherhood Among Muslims
6. The Prophet Muhammad's Morals

Instructions

- A poem is preferred over an essay.
- Pick a topic that you feel connected to.
- The poem should be between 4 and 8 lines.
- The Essay should be between 6 and 10 lines.
- The central message of the event or topic should be focused on.

Chapter 22

Morals and Character of Prophet Muhammad

In this chapter, we will discuss some of the gems from the life of Prophet Muhammad that show his elevated character as a human being.

He was the Messenger of God

- First and foremost, he was the Messenger of God. His entire life and status in Islam must be looked at in the light of this fact.
- Calling the Messenger a great statesman, political leader, army commander, or anything else reduces his primary position, i.e., the Messenger of God.
- He fought wars, led armies, and formed a government because God commanded him to do so, to fulfill his mission. He had no desire or aims for it.
- He was an ultimate role model of ethics and morality in all these positions. Due to his position as a Messenger of God, he accomplished his goals in only 23 years.

Quran's testimony about him

وَ اِنَّكَ لَعَلٰى خُلُقٍ عَظِيمٍ

And indeed, you are on the exalted standard of character (Qalam:4)

وَ مَآ اَرْسَلْنٰكَ اِلَّا رَحْمَةً لِّلْعٰلَمِينَ

We have sent you not but as a Mercy to the worlds (Al Anbiya:107)

لَقَدْ كَانَ لَكُمْ فِىْ رَسُوْلِ اللّٰهِ اُسْوَةٌ حَسَنَةٌ

(People) Indeed, you have, in the Messenger of Allah, a great example to follow (Ahzab:21)

لَقَدْ جَآءَكُمْ رَسُوْلٌ مِّنْ اَنْفُسِكُمْ عَزِيْزٌ عَلَيْهِ مَا عَنِتُّمْ حَرِيْصٌ عَلَيْكُمْ بِالْمُؤْمِنِيْنَ رَءُوْفٌ رَحِيْمٌ

Indeed, a messenger has come to you from among you, your distress grieves him, wishes your betterment, and he is forgiving and merciful for the believers (Tawbah: 128)

Testimony of his beloved wife

- One of his wives, Ayesha, was once asked about his character and she said:

فَإِنَّ خُلُقَ نَبِّي اللّٰهِ صَلَّى اللّٰهُ عَلَيْهِ وَسَلَّمَ كَانَ الْقُرْآن

Indeed, the character of the Prophet was the Quran [Sahih Muslim #746]

His Character

Merciful to human beings

- Anas Bin Maalik reported: While we were in the masjid with the Prophet, a Bedouin came, not knowing the etiquette of the mosque, and he urinated in the mosque. The Companions reproached him and tried to grab him. The Prophet said, "Leave him and let him finish." They left him alone until he finished urinating. The Prophet then called him over and said, "Any kind of urine or filth is not suitable for these mosques. Instead, they are only built for the remembrance of God, the Prayer, and the recitation of the Quran." He then asked someone to bring a bucket of water, and he poured it over the affected area of the mosque. [Sahih Muslim #285]

- He was an easy-going person and loved to cover up other people's faults. Anas said, "I served the Prophet for 10 years. And whenever he sent me on an errand that I was unable to complete, he never said, 'Why did you not do it? Rather, 'It would have been completed if God had decided to complete it." He never even said Uff to me, and if I did something wrong, he never said, 'Why did you do that?' [Masnad Ahmad #352, Sahih Al Bukhari #6038]

- The Prophet once said, " If one provides for, takes care of, and raises an orphan, regardless of whether the orphan is a relative, then I and he will be like these two in Paradise." He joined his index and middle fingers together when saying that. [Sahih Muslim #2983]

Merciful to animals

- Ibn Masud reported that once, while we were on a journey with the Prophet of Allah, he went away from the camp to relieve himself. Meanwhile, we saw a small red bird with two chicks. We then took the bird's chick to play with them. When the bird saw that, it came down, flapping its wings frantically, and drew near to the ground. When the Prophet came and saw that, he sadly asked, "Who has troubled this bird by taking its chicks? Return them to her." (Hadith)

- Jabir bin Abdullah reported that the Prophet passed by a donkey that had been branded on its face. Branding was the Arab practice of making a permanent mark on an animal by burning it with a hot iron to identify it. The Prophet looked at the donkey and said, "May Allah curse the one who has done this with this animal." (Sahih Muslim #2117)

Grateful servant of God

- He never spoke badly of any food. Instead, if he liked a particular dish, he would eat it and appreciate it. If he did not, he would leave it and would not eat, but would never say anything negative about the food. (Seerah)

- The Prophet did not merely tell people about the importance of prayers. Instead, he prayed himself, especially at night, to the point that his feet would swell and develop cracks. Once, his wife, Aisha, asked if God had already forgiven him for his past and future sins. "Why do you pray so much?" He replied:

أَفَلَا أَكُونُ عَبْدًا شَكُورًا

"Shall I not be a grateful servant?" (Sahih Al Bukhari #1130)

A loving family man

- He used to mend his own shoes, patch his garments, milk sheep, and even help his wives with house chores. (Seerah)

- Abu Huraira reported: One day, an old companion saw the Prophet kissing his grandson Al-Hasan. The companion said, "I have ten children, and I have never shown affection to any of them." The Prophet said, "Verily, whoever does not show mercy will not receive mercy." (Sahih Al Bukhari #5651)

- Abu Buraidah reported that the Messenger of God was delivering a Khutbah to us when Al-Hasan and Al-Hussain (his grandchildren) came, wearing red shirts, walking, and stumbling on the way. The Prophet came down from the pulpit, took them with him, made them sit before him, and then continued his Khutbah. (Seerah)

- The Prophet spent 25 years with his first wife, Khadijah. He used to love her deeply and honor her even after her passing. If a gift was sent to Prophet Muhammad or he slaughtered an animal in the house, he would not hesitate to share it with a friend or relative of Khadijah in response to the kindness and compassion that Khadijah showed to him during her life (Seerah)

A humble man

- Abu Masood reported that one day, a man came from a faraway place to meet with and speak to the Prophet of God. The man was in complete awe of the Prophet after meeting him. He was so nervous that he was shaking. Noticing the man's nervousness, the Prophet put him at ease by saying, "Calm down, for I am not a king. I am nothing more than the son of a woman who used to eat Al Qadid (salted meat that has been dried in the sun) in this rocky, barren land (Hadith)

- Despite being the leader of a nation when Muslims ruled the Arabian Peninsula, he continued to live a modest and humble life. One day, Umar bin Khattab visited him while he was sleeping. When he woke up and sat, Umar saw marks on the straw mat that it had left on one side of his body. The Prophet began to rub that side of his body. When Umar noticed this, he began to cry and asked the Prophet to get him a better and more comfortable bed. The Prophet replied:

  "What do I have to do with this world? Verily, the example of me and this world is nothing other than the example of a rider or traveler who has traveled on a scorching, hot day. That rider seeks shade under a tree for an hour during the day and then gets up and leaves for the destination" (Al-Tirmidhi 2/280)

A moderate person

- A group of three men came to the houses of the Prophet's wives, asking how the Prophet worships. When they were informed, they considered their worship insufficient and said, "Where are we from the Prophet, as his past and future sins have been forgiven?" Then one of them said,

- "I will offer the prayer throughout the night forever."

- The other said, "I will fast throughout the year and not break my fast."

- The third said, "I will keep away from the women and will not marry forever."

- When the Prophet heard that, he came to them and said, "Are you the same people who said something like this? By Allah, I am more submissive to Allah and more afraid of Him than you; yet I fast and break my fast, I do sleep, and I also marry women. So, he who does not follow my tradition in religion is not from my religion (meaning you should be moderate and balanced in your life) (Hadith)

- The Prophet said, "Make religious things easy for the people, and do not make it difficult for them, and give them the good news about God and do not push them away from religion (by creating difficulties for them)." (Sahih Al Bukhari 8/73/146)

Friendly

- There was a man from the people of the desert, Zahir Ibn Haram, who was not very good-looking. The Prophet used to love him. The Prophet saw Zahir one day in the market where he was selling his goods. The Prophet quietly walked towards and embraced him from behind so Zahir could not see who it was. The Prophet may have placed his hands over his eyes. Zahir asked: "Who is this?" Instead of answering him, the Prophet jokingly said, "Who is going to buy this slave?" Then Zahir said, "O Prophet of Allah, who is going to buy me? I am worthless." The Prophet said, "No, but with Allah, you are priceless." (Seerah)

Forgiving

- One of the people who did the Prophet much harm over a long period was Abdullah ibn Ubayy, the chief of the hypocrites in Medinah. He spoke ill of the Prophet, spread false rumors about him and his family, left with his supporters the Muslim army shortly before a crucial battle, cooperated with the enemies of Islam, and plotted against the Muslim state. Nevertheless, before his death, he requested that the Prophet lead his funeral prayer. Umar ibn Al-Khattab reports:

- "When Abdullah ibn Ubayy died, the Prophet was asked to pray for him. When the Prophet stood up to do so, I jumped to him and said: 'Prophet of God! Will you pray for Ibn Ubayy while he says this and that? I reminded him of what the man said. The Prophet smiled and said, ' Leave me alone, Umar.' But when I was too persistent, he said, ' I have been given a choice, and I made my choice. Had I known that if I prayed for his forgiveness over 70 times, God would forgive him, I would certainly do so.' He then offered the funeral prayer for him and left. It was not long before two verses of Surah 9 were revealed, stating: 'You shall not pray for any of them who dies, and you shall not stand by his grave. For they have denied God and His Messenger and died as hardened sinners.'" (Surah Tawbah: 84)

His mission as a role model

I have been sent to perfect good moral character (Hadith Al Muwatta #1614)

What is the best way to show our love for the Prophet?

ALLAH

- Throughout this course in L3 and in L2 before, we learned various attributes of Allah, and this is the time to summarize what we have learned from these two levels.

- It is clear that if we want to know more about our God, Allah, we should learn the life of Prophet Muhammad.

- Allah was with the Prophet throughout his journey of life, before and after the Prophethood.

- However, Allah is only visible (through His attributes) in our lives when we live according to His teachings. Meaning we should try to live the Quran as the Prophet did.

- If we know Allah through His attributes properly and how He deals with us, then no bad circumstance or situation can make us sad, and similarly, no good circumstance or situation can make us arrogant.

- Because we know it's all from Allah, and He is testing us in this world and will reward us in the next life.

SEERAH ACTIVITY

Create a Madani Seerah Timeline

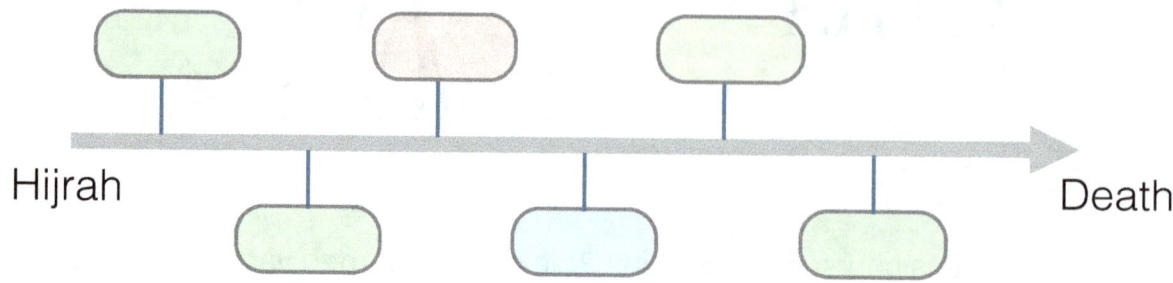

Hijrah

Death

Instructions

1. Create a visual timeline of Seerah (Madani) using:
   a. Index cards
   b. Poster
   c. Digital tools like Canva or Google Slides
2. You can draw, paste pictures, or write short summaries for key events.
3. Specify the period of the timeline.
4. Identify key events that you consider important.
5. Events must be in the correct time order.
6. Mark the approximate date and specific location for the events.
7. Make it visually appealing.